EVERYMAN'S
BOOK OF
SEA SONGS

EVERYMAN'S
BOOK OF
SEA SONGS

Richard Baker
&
Antony Miall

J M Dent & Sons Ltd
London Melbourne Toronto

First published 1982
© Richard Baker and Antony Miall 1982

This book is set in 12/13½ Monophoto Sabon
Printed and made in Great Britain by Butler & Tanner Ltd,
Frome and London for
J. M. Dent & Sons Ltd
Aldine House, 33 Welbeck Street, London W1M 8LX

British Library Cataloguing in Publication Data

Everyman's book of sea songs.
    1. Sea songs
    I. Baker, Richard, 1925-   II. Miall, Antony
    784.6'86238   M1977.S2

    ISBN 0-460-04470-2

CONTENTS

CONTENTS

ACKNOWLEDGEMENTS

The authors and publisher would like to thank the following for their kind permission to reproduce the illustrations in this book:

BBC Hulton Picture Library   frontispiece, p. 1
National Maritime Museum   pp. viii, 55, 81, 139, 183

INTRODUCTION

As a nation we have always needed sailors, and we have long celebrated them in song, though often without the slightest idea of the realities of life at sea. The sailor himself is a sceptical fellow who has no time for such romantic nonsense from others, though he is by no means above boasting about himself and his ship. Thus over the centuries, ashore and afloat, there has grown up a great mass of songs in praise of the sailor's life. Against them must be set the improvised ballads in which men expressed their resentment at the terrible conditions of their existence, accounts of appalling sufferings in battle, and the work songs which for all their melodic beauty, bear witness to the gruelling labour required, day and night, to keep the great sailing ships of bygone days at sea.

Then there are the songs of love, whether of sailors themselves, or directed by sweethearts ashore to their loved ones far away. Some are deeply felt, others are the expression of passing fancies, and extol the easy-come-easy-go attitude to love traditionally possessed by some sailors and by some of their girlfriends.

There are songs of homecoming, dreams or celebrations; of landfall after a long voyage. Sometimes the harbours have a geographical location and a name, sometimes the writer – especially a Victorian one – seizes on the great potential of the sea as a metaphor for the uncertainties of human existence, and points us towards the Heavenly anchorage which sooner or later affords permanent shelter for the storm-tossed soul. More attractive, because more natural, are laments for individual sailors; for Tom who has gone to Hilo, and Dibdin's immortal Tom Bowling, mourned by the entire crew now that he has 'gone aloft'.

Examples of many other kinds of sea song will be found in this book. It contains much familiar material, but also songs that were new to us when we came across them. Well-known or otherwise, they are all eminently *singable*, and that has been a main consideration in making our selection. For the fact is that sailors do still sing. Certainly in the Royal Navy they do. There's no need any longer to heave the capstan round to the encouragement of a rhythmic shanty, but equivalents of the old foc'sle ditties still very much exist, made up by more or less ingenious rhymesters – most of them too esoteric or too explicit for publication in a volume of this kind! Part of the fun of them is that they belong to a sailor's personal baggage and can only be shared with mates in the know.

Our belief is that the songs will be especially enjoyed by those who go to sea in craft large or small, that they may well provide material for those home-made entertainments which have always been part of the life of the sailor. Where appropriate we have indicated chords for that universal instrument, the guitar. But as often as not the songs will be sung as no doubt they were originally, with no accompaniment, or at best with a mouth organ or squeeze-box. However, the sailor, or would-be sailor, ashore, is not forgotten. For him, with his assumed access to the parlour piano, there are a number of ballads from days gone by to stir his landlocked being with a whiff of the old briny.

1

A LIFE ON
THE OCEAN WAVE!

When the sailor is not positively in danger, he is often extremely uncomfortable, even today, and in days gone by his life must have been almost perpetually disagreeable. It is therefore hard to understand why his existence has so often been thought ideal. Few writers were actually motivated by the call for naval recruits – even Charles Dibdin who was rewarded by a grateful government for making the sea service appear so attractive during the Napoleonic wars. Freedom figures largely among the supposed attractions of a life 'on the flashing brine', while English gentlemen who prefer to 'sleep safe in their beds' are shown to be a dull, unambitious lot who care overmuch for the safety they enjoy at the expense of their braver countrymen.

The sailor, on the other hand, is characteristically endowed with courage, generosity, even-temper, good humour, tolerance, patriotism and constancy, and is often credited with a tendency to sing and dance on all occasions, even when the stormy winds do blow and the enemy's broadsides are crashing through the rigging. But we must not be cynical. Through learning to share the perils and confinement of life afloat with others, Jack often does become a better citizen than most. By and large he merits the praise bestowed on him in the ten songs which follow and some of the landsmen's ditties have, after all, had the honour of serving at sea themselves: *Heart of Oak* was played as Nelson's ships went into action off Trafalgar.

THE TRUE ENGLISH SAILOR

Written and composed by CHARLES DIBDIN

Jack __ dan - ces and sings, and is al - ways con-tent; In his
vows to his lass he'll ne'er fail her, His an - chor's a trip when his

Tho' care-less and head-long, if
dan-ger should press, And rank'd 'mongst the free list of ro - vers, Yet he'll
melt in-to tears at a tale of dis-tress, He'll melt in-to tears at a
tale of dis-tress, And prove the most con-stant of lo - vers, And

THE TRUE ENGLISH SAILOR

1.   Jack dances and sings and is always content;
      In his vows to his lass he'll ne'er fail her,
      His anchor's a trip when his money's all spent,
      And this is the life of a sailor.

2.   Alert in his duty, he readily flies
      Where winds the tired vessel are flinging;
      Though sunk to the sea-gods or toss'd to the skies,
      Still Jack is found working and singing.

3.   'Long side of an enemy, boldly and brave
      He'll with broadside and broadside regale her;
      Yet he'll sigh from his soul o'er that enemy's grave,
      So noble's the mind of a sailor.

4.   Let cannons roar loud, burst their sides let the bombs,
      Let the winds a dread hurricane rattle.
      The rough and the pleasant he takes as it comes,
      And laughs at the storm and the battle.

5.   In a fostering pow'r while Jack puts his trust,
      As fortune comes smiling he'll hail her,
      Resign'd still and manly, since what must be, must,
      And this is the mind of a sailor.

6.   Tho' careless and headlong, if danger should press,
      And rank'd 'mongst the free list of rovers,
      Yet he'll melt into tears at a tale of distress,
      And prove the most constant of lovers.

7.   To rancour unknown, to no passion a slave,
      Nor unmanly, nor mean, nor a railer;
      He's gentle as mercy, as fortitude brave,
      And this is a true English sailor.

A characteristic eighteenth-century sea song, 'The True English Sailor' was
written and composed by Charles Dibdin the elder (1745-1814) whose sailor
songs were believed by Napoleon to have done more for British naval glory
than all Nelson's bravery. His hundreds of songs won him recognition and a
pension of £200 per annum from the government, but inefficient copyright
laws lost him many times that amount in pirated songs and poems. A full
biography of Dibdin appears on page 143.

A LIFE ON THE OCEAN WAVE

Written by EPES SARGENT

Composed by HENRY RUSSELL

A LIFE ON THE OCEAN WAVE!

1. A life on the ocean wave!
   A home on the rolling deep!
   Where the scatter'd waters rave,
   And the winds their revels keep!
   Like an eagle cag'd I pine,
   On this dull unchanging shore,
   Oh! give me the flashing brine,
   The spray and the tempest's roar,
   A life on the ocean wave! etc.

2. Once more on the deck I stand
   Of my own swift gliding craft,
   Set sail! farewell to the land,
   The gale follows fair abaft.
   We shoot thro' the sparkling foam,
   Like an ocean-bird set free,
   Like the ocean-bird, our home
   We'll find far out on the sea!
   A life on the ocean wave! etc.

3. The land is no longer in view,
   The clouds have begun to frown,
   But with a stout vessel and crew
   We'll say, let the storm come down!
   And the song of our hearts shall be
   While the winds and the waters rave,
   A life on the heaving sea!
   A home on the bounding wave!
   A life on the ocean wave! etc.

The words of 'A Life on the Ocean Wave!' were presented to the composer, Henry Russell, by the poet after they had been rejected by a publisher. Russell, an Englishman by birth, was seeking his fortune in America and took the manuscript of the poem into a Broadway music store where, in his own words: 'I was invited into a back room where there was a capital piano. I hummed an air or two, ran my fingers over the keys, then stopped, feeling baffled; suddenly an idea struck me and presently touching the keys with a confident exclamation, that bright little air rang out which is now so well known.'

Russell's career was full of small successes and highly popular songs such as 'Cheer Boys, Cheer!' and 'Woodman, Spare that Tree!' None, however, achieved such lasting fame as 'A Life on the Ocean Wave!' which has been the official march of the Royal Marines since 1889.

RULE, BRITANNIA!

Written by JAMES THOMSON

Composed by THOMAS AUGUSTINE ARNE

1.When Bri - tain first___ at Heav'n's com-mand, A-

- rose _____ from out the a - zure main, A-rose, a-rose, a-rose from out the

CHORUS

Rule, Bri-tannia! Bri-tan-nia, rule the waves;   Britons ne - ver will be slaves.

G7   C   G7 Ami   A7 D   D7   G D7 G D G C   G D7 G

RULE, BRITANNIA!

1. When Britain first at Heav'n's command
    Arose from out the azure main;
    This was the charter of the land,
    And guardian angels sang this strain:

CHORUS   Rule, Britannia! Britannia, rule the waves:
          Britons never will be slaves.

2. The nations not so blest as thee,
    Shall in their turns to tyrants fall;
    While thou shalt flourish great and free,
    The dread and envy of them all.

CHORUS   Rule, Britannia! etc.

3. Still more majestic shalt thou rise,
    More dreadful from each foreign stroke;

> As the loud blast that tears the skies,
> Serves but to root thy native oak.

CHORUS   Rule, Britannia! etc.

4.   Thee haughty tyrants ne'er shall tame,
       All their attempts to bend thee down
       Will but arouse thy generous flame;
       But work their woe, and thy renown.

CHORUS   Rule, Britannia! etc.

5.   To thee belongs the rural reign;
       Thy cities shall with commerce shine;
       All thine shall be the subject main,
       And every shore it circles thine.

CHORUS   Rule, Britannia! etc.

6.   The Muses, still with freedom found,
       Shall to thy happy coast repair;
       Blest Isle! with matchless beauty crown'd,
       And manly hearts to guide the fair.

CHORUS   Rule, Britannia! etc.

Composed by Thomas Augustine Arne in 1740 for his masque *Alfred*, 'Rule, Britannia!' was first heard at a performance given at Cliefden House, Maidenhead – then the residence of Frederick, Prince of Wales – when the masque was given to celebrate the accession of George I and the birthday of the Princess Augusta. This most popular of all English national airs was first heard in London in 1745 and achieved instant popularity. So well known was it that Handel even quoted it in his *Occasional Oratorio* in the following year when it was sung to the words, 'War shall cease, welcome peace!'.

Predictably 'Rule, Britannia!' was seized upon by the Jacobites and James Thomson's words were altered accordingly:

> 'Britannia, rouse at Heav'n's command!
> And crown thy native Prince again;
> Then Peace shall bless thy happy land,
> And plenty pour in from the main:
> Then shalt thou be – Britannia, thou shalt be
> From home and foreign tyrants free.

Behold, great Charles! thy godlike son,
With majesty and sweetness crowned;
His worth th'admiring world doth own,
And fame's loud trump proclaims the sound.
Thy captain him, Britannia, him declare!
Of kings and heroes he's the heir.

Then, Britons, rouse! with trumpets' sound
Proclaim this solemn, happy day'.
Let mirth with cheerful music crowned
Drive sullen thoughts and cares away!
Come, Britons, sing! Britannia, draw thy sword!
And use it for thy rightful lord!'

Anyone who has sung or heard 'Rule, Britannia!' sung at the Last Night of the Proms cannot doubt its staying power. It is still Britain's second national anthem – and deservedly so.

YOU GENTLEMEN OF ENGLAND

Written by MARTIN PARKS

Traditional melody.

gen-tle-men of Eng-land, Who live at home at ease, How lit-tle do you

think up-on The dan-gers of the seas: Give ear unto the mariners, And

G   B   Emi   A   D   A   D   Emi

they will plainly show, All the cares, and the fears, When the storm-y winds do

D   Ami   D   G   Ami D   G   D

CHORUS

blow; All the cares, and the fears, When the storm-y winds do

G   G   Ami   D   G   D

blow.

p   *f*

G

YOU GENTLEMEN OF ENGLAND

1. You gentlemen of England,
    That live at home at ease,
    How little do you think upon
    The dangers of the seas;
    Give ear unto the mariners,
    And they will plainly show
    All the cares and the fears
    When the stormy winds do blow.

2. The sailor must have courage,
    No danger must he shun;
    In every kind of weather
    His course he still must run;
    Now mounted on the top-mast,
    How dreadful 'tis below:
    Then we ride, as the tide,
    When the stormy winds do blow.

3. If enemies oppose us,
    And England is at war
    With any foreign nation,
    We fear not wound nor scar.
    To humble them, come on, lads,
    Their flags we'll soon lay low;
    Clear the way for the fray,
    Tho' the stormy winds do blow.

4. Sometimes in Neptune's bosom
    Our ship is toss'd by waves,
    And every man expecting
    The sea to be our graves;
    Then up aloft she's mounted,
    And down again so low,
    In the waves, on the seas,
    When the stormy winds do blow.

5. But when the danger's over,
    And safe we come on shore,
    The horrors of the tempest
    We think of then no more;

The flowing bowl invites us,
And joyfully we go
All the day drink away,
Tho' the stormy winds do blow.

A well-known sea song of the seventeenth century, 'You Gentlemen of England' is perhaps even better known by its last line – 'While the stormy winds do blow'. It first appeared in 1686. In one collection of the period the song has the following descriptive heading: 'The praise of sailors here set forth, with their hard fortunes which doe befall them on the seas, when landmen sleep safe in their beds: to a pleasant new tune.' The tune is certainly pleasant but the present editors thought it not quite pleasant enough to be sustained through the original fourteen verses that appear in the Ritson manuscript. So we limit ourselves to five!

WE BE THREE POOR MARINERS

Words and music : Traditional

Moderato

1. We be three poor ma - ri - ners, New - ly__ come from the sea ; We spend our lives in jeo - par - dy, While o - thers live at ease. Shall we go dance the round, the round, the round? Shall

we _ go dance the round, the round, the round? And he that is a

Ab   Eb   Ab   Bb

bul - ly boy, Come pledge me on _ this ground, a-ground, a-ground.

Eb   Ab   Bb   Eb

WE BE THREE POOR MARINERS

1. We be three poor mariners,
   Newly come from the seas;
   We spend our lives in jeopardy,

While others live at ease.
Shall we go dance the round?
Shall we go dance the round?
And he that is a jolly boy,
Come pledge me on this ground.

2.   We care not for those martial men
That do our states disdain;
But we care for the merchantmen
Who do our states maintain.
To them we dance this round.
To them we dance this round.
And he that is a jolly boy,
Come pledge me on this ground.

One of the earliest songs in the collection, 'We be three poor Mariners' first appeared in *Deuteromalia* – Thomas Ravenscroft's second collection of rounds and catches etc. published in 1609. It is also found in a manuscript of Scottish melodies of about 1630 where it is given in lute tablature. 'We be three poor Mariners' was sung to one of the best loved dance tunes of the seventeenth century – a period when the English were known on the continent as 'The Dancing English'. It is interesting to find sailors already deeming themselves superior to mere soldiers!

HEART OF OAK

Written by DAVID GARRICK

Composed by WILLIAM BOYCE

1. Come cheer up, my lads, 'tis to

glo - ry we steer, To add something new to this won - derful year, To

hon- our we call you, not press you like slaves, For who are so free as the

F7   Bb   F

sons of the waves. Heart of oak are our ships, jol-ly tars are our men, we

p

C   F   Bb

ad lib.   *a tempo*

al - ways are ready,   steady, boys, steady,   We'll fight and will con-quer a-

colla voce   *cresc.*

Cmi D   Gmi   Bb   Eb   C7

- gain and a - gain.

sf >   > p   > ff   sf > >

F   F7   Bb

HEART OF OAK

1.   Come cheer up, my lads, 'tis to glory we steer,
    To add something more to this wonderful year,
    To honour we call you, not press you like slaves,
    For who are so free as the sons of the waves?

CHORUS   Heart of oak are our ships,
           Jolly tars are our men,
           We always are ready,
           Steady, boys, steady,
           We'll fight and we'll conquer again and again.

2.   We ne'er see our foes but we wish them to stay,
    They never see us but they wish us away,
    If they run, why we follow, and run them ashore,
    And if they won't fight us, we cannot do more.

CHORUS   Heart of oak are our ships,
           Jolly tars are our men,
           We always are ready,
           Steady, boys, steady,
           We'll fight and we'll conquer again and again.

3.   They swear they'll invade us, these terrible foes,
    They frighten our women, our children and beaus,
    But should their flat bottoms in darkness get o'er,
    Still Britons they'll find to receive them on shore.

CHORUS   Heart of oak are our ships,
           Jolly tars are our men,
           We always are ready,
           Steady, boys, steady,
           We'll fight and we'll conquer again and again.

The words of this most popular English sea song were written by David Garrick and the music is by Dr Boyce. It was first performed by a Mr Champnes in *Harlequin's Invasion* (1759) and immediately became successful. The fine sweeping melodic line and the stirring words have always made 'Heart of Oak' a firm favourite with the English, but it had, apparently, fans from further afield. Boswell, in his visit to Corsica, was asked by the natives to sing an English song. He responded with 'Heart of Oak': 'Never did I see men so delighted with a song as the Corsicans were with "Heart of Oak" ... "Cuore di querco," they cried, "Bravo Inglese!" It was quite a joyous riot. I fancied myself to be a recruiting sea-officer – I fancied all my chorus of Corsicans aboard the British fleet.'

SPANISH LADIES

Words and Music: Traditional [arr.A.M.]

SOLO

1.Fare - well and a - dieu un-to

you Span-ish la-dies, Fare - well and a - dieu to you la - dies of

Spain; For it's we've re-ceived or-ders for to sail for old England But we

CHORUS

hope ve - ry soon we shall see you a - gain. We'll rant and we'll

ro - ar like true Brit - ish sai - lors, We'll rant and we'll roar a -

- cross the salt seas, Un - til we strike soun-dings in the Channel of old

Eng-land From Ush-ant to Scil - ly is thir-ty - five leagues.

SPANISH LADIES

1. Farewell and adieu unto you Spanish ladies,
    Farewell and adieu to you ladies of Spain;
    For it's we've received orders for to sail for old England,
    But we hope very soon we shall see you again.

CHORUS   We'll rant and we'll roar like true British sailors,
          We'll rant and we'll roar across the salt seas,
          Until we strike soundings in the Channel of old England,
          From Ushant to Scilly is thirty-five leagues.

2. Then we hove our ship to the wind at sou'-west, my boys,
    We hove our ship to our soundings for to see;
    So we rounded and sounded, and got forty-five fathoms,
    We squared our main yard, up channel steered we.

CHORUS   We'll rant and we'll roar like true British sailors,
          We'll rant and we'll roar across the salt seas,
          Until we strike soundings in the Channel of old England,
          From Ushant to Scilly is thirty-five leagues.

3. Now the first land we made it is called the Deadman,
    Then Ram Head off Plymouth, Start, Portland and Wight;
    We sailed by Beachy, by Fairlee and Dungeness,
    Until we came abreast of the South Foreland Light.

CHORUS   We'll rant and we'll roar like true British sailors,
          We'll rant and we'll roar across the salt seas,
          Until we strike soundings in the Channel of old England,
          From Ushant to Scilly is thirty-five leagues.

4. Then the signal was made for the grand fleet for to anchor,
    All in the downs that night for to meet;
    Then it's stand by your stoppers, let go your shank painters,
    Haul all your clew garnets, stick out tacks and sheets.

CHORUS   We'll rant and we'll roar like true British sailors,
          We'll rant and we'll roar across the salt seas,
          Until we strike soundings in the Channel of old England,
          From Ushant to Scilly is thirty-five leagues.

5. Now let every man toss off a full bumper,
    And let every man toss off a full bowl;

And we'll drink and be merry and drown melancholy,
Singing, here's a good health to all true-hearted souls.

CHORUS   We'll rant and we'll roar like true British sailors,
We'll rant and we'll roar across the salt seas,
Until we strike soundings in the Channel of old England,
From Ushant to Scilly is thirty-five leagues.

William Chappell in his exhaustive *Popular Music of the Olden Time* gives this ballad under the heading 'Traditional Tunes of Uncertain Date'. The number of variants, however, suggest that it really is very old indeed. Of all the versions that exist, the one in the major key given here is probably the best known nowadays.

For its topographical lyrics, 'Spanish Ladies' is fascinating and gives a vivid picture of ships under sail in the English Channel. The 'Grand Fleet' was the old name for the Channel Fleet, 'Deadman' and 'Fairlee' are sea names for Dodman Point near Plymouth and Fairlight Hill near Hastings, and Ushant is the Ile d'Ouessant off Brest in France.

Two variants of the last line are interesting. The first states: 'But we hope very soon we shall see you again' and the second: 'And perhaps never more we shall see you again' – obviously two different batches of Spanish Ladies!

OVER THE HARBOR BAR

Written by FRANK W. PRATT

Composed by GODFREY MARKS

1. Here's a song, jol-ly lads, you can join in, For our ship's with-in sight of the bar; ____ No more need your hearts be a -

CHORUS

OVER THE HARBOR BAR

1. Here's a song, jolly lads, you can join in,
    For our ship's within sight of the bar;
    No more need your hearts be a-pining,
    For the smiles of your sweethearts afar.
    Many weeks o'er the waves we've been dancing,
    Strange lands and fair faces have seen,
    But naught far and near so entrancing
    As the shores of our island so green.

CHORUS And it's over the harbor bar, boys,
        Over the harbor bar,
        There's a welcome sweet,
        With smiles to greet,
        Over the harbor bar.

2. We've sailed thro' the bluest of water,
   And quaffed of the richest of wine,
   We've danced with Spain's sunny daughter,
   But for Nancy at home we pine.
   And oft when the tempests are blowing,
   Our thoughts, they will wander afar,
   To the hearts that with fondness are glowing,
   And waiting just over the bar.

CHORUS   And it's over the harbor bar, boys,
          Over the harbor bar,
          There's a welcome sweet,
          With smiles to greet,
          Over the harbor bar.

3. When we've done with the water a-wrestling,
   And our timbers show signs of decay,
   In a cot 'neath the white cliffs a-nestling,
   The bos'n's last call we'll obey.
   Looking hard at the bright star of morning,
   We'll steer for the harbor afar,
   And at last the great Pilot's glad warning,
   Will be heard as we're nearing the bar.

CHORUS   And it's over the harbor bar, boys,
          Over the harbor bar,
          There's a welcome sweet,
          With smiles to greet,
          Over the harbor bar.

This ballad comes from late nineteenth-century America and has all the bounce and flourish of Tin Pan Alley. Godfrey Marks had a special line in sea songs and his 'Sailing' (1883) enjoyed enormous popularity with its swinging chorus and satisfying last line 'When Jack comes home again'. 'Over the Harbor Bar' is just as telling in performance and will repay a spirited rendering with everyone joining in the chorus!

THE LIFEBOAT CREW

Written by JOHN HARTLEY

Composed by WILLIAM PARKINSON

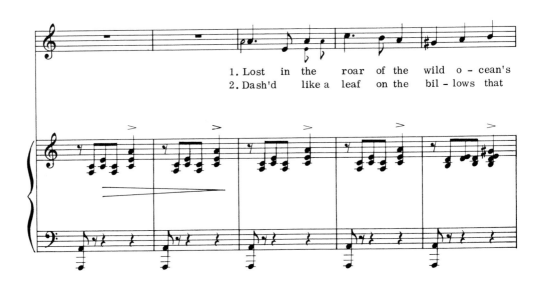

1. Lost in the roar of the wild o-cean's
2. Dash'd like a leaf on the bil-lows that

rage,   Are the   cries   of the   ti – mid and   brave; _____
roar,   Now   lost   in the   wild dash – ing   spray, _____

Fear-less   the   crew   of the   life – boat   en – gage,   The   tem – pest-toss'd
Trem-bling with   fear   stands the   crowd on   the   shore,   Some   weep – ing, some

ves – sel   to   save. _____   Hark   to the   thunder   that
striv-ing   to   pray, _____   Mothers and   wives,   mute with

shakes   heav'n's dome,   See   how   the fierce lightnings flash   by; _____
an-guish stand   by,   Yet   proud of their   dear ones so   brave, _____

con espressione

With a cheer and a pray'r for the lov'd ones at home, Go the
Strain-ing their ears to catch sound of that cry, Which at

rall.   *con spirito*

he - roes to do or to die. _____ Hail! to the
last faint-ly comes o'er the wave. _____

life - boat, God bless the brave crew, Who dare the tem -

- pest - u - ous wave. _____ Strengthen and

bless the hearts dar – ing and true, Who risk all to

suc – cour and save. _____

3. Loud ring the cheers as the life – boat re –

– turns, Forms drip – ping with foam and with rain; _____

Grate-ful and   proud   eve-ry bo - som now   burns,   They have

con - quer'd old   o - cean a - gain. _____

Then   who   will for - bear to   lend

help - ing   hand,   To the   life - sav - ing   boat   and   its

crew, _____ Whose cour-age and pluck makes us

proud of the land, That boasts men so fear-less and

con spirito

true. _____ Hail! to the life - boat, God

bless the brave crew, Who dare the tem -

-pest - u - ous   wave. _____

Strength- en   and   bless   the hearts   dar - ing   and

true,   Who   risk   all   to   suc - cour   and

save. _____

Fine

ff

THE LIFEBOAT CREW

1. Lost in the roar of the wild ocean's rage,
    Are the cries of the timid and brave:
    Fearless the crew of the lifeboat engage,
    The tempest toss'd vessel to save.
    Hark to the thunder that shakes heav'n's dome,
    See how the fierce lightnings flash by;
    With a cheer and a pray'r for the lov'd ones at home,
    Go the heroes to do or to die.

CHORUS   Hail! to the lifeboat,
    God bless the brave crew,
    Who dare the tempestuous wave.
    Strengthen and bless the hearts daring and true,
    Who risk all to succour and save.

2. Dash'd like a leaf on the billows that roar,
    Now lost in the wild dashing spray,
    Trembling with fear stands the crowd on the shore,
    Some weeping, some striving to pray.
    Mothers and wives, mute with anguish stand by,
    Yet proud of the dear ones so brave,
    Straining their ears to catch sound of that cry,
    Which at last faintly comes o'er the wave.

CHORUS   Hail! to the lifeboat,
    God bless the brave crew,
    Who dare the tempestuous wave.
    Strengthen and bless the hearts daring and true,
    Who risk all to succour and save.

3. Loud ring the cheers as the lifeboat returns,
    Forms dripping with foam and with rain;
    Grateful and proud every bosom now burns,
    They have conquer'd old ocean again.
    Then who will forbear to lend helping hand,
    To the life-saving boat and its crew,
    Whose courage and pluck makes us proud of the land,
    That boasts men so fearless and true.

CHORUS   Hail! to the lifeboat,
    God bless the brave crew,

Who dare the tempestuous wave.
Strengthen and bless the hearts daring and true,
Who risk all to succour and save.

Songs about lifeboats were popular parlour fare in the nineteenth century when singing about the terrors of the sea behind cosy velvet curtains helped to reinforce a feeling of security. One of the best-known lifeboat songs was written by Ciro Pinsuti to words by George R. Sims:

'Been out in the lifeboat often? Ay, ay, sir, oft enough.
When it's rougher than this? Lor' bless you! this ain't what we calls rough!'

John Hartley's words may not conjure up so vivid a picture, but they are very much in the spirit of jingoism frequently found in drawing-room sea songs:

'Who will forbear to lend helping hand,
To the life-saving boat and its crew,
Whose courage and pluck makes us proud of the land,
That boasts men so fearless and true?'

'The Lifeboat Crew' is quite simply one of the best 'sings' in its class. The present editors find a nip of rum improves the verse, but the chorus needs no bush!

THE SEA IS ENGLAND'S GLORY

Written by J.W. LAKE

Composed by STEPHEN GLOVER

Allegro con spirito

1. The sea is Eng-land's glo-ry! The bound-ing waves her

C7   F   Fdim F

THE SEA IS ENGLAND'S GLORY!

1. The sea is England's glory!
    The bounding waves her throne;
    For ages bright in story,
    The ocean is her own.
    In war the first, the fearless
    Her standard leads the brave,
    In peace she reigns so peerless,
    The Empress of the wave!

2. The sea is England's splendour!
    Her wealth the mighty main;
    She is the world's defender;
    The humble to sustain;
    Her gallant sons in story

Stand bravest of the brave,
Oh! England's strength and glory
Are on her ocean wave!

3.   Thou loveliest land of beauty!
Where dwells domestic worth,
Where loyalty and duty
Entwine each heart and hearth!
Thy rock is freedom's pillow
The rampart of the brave,
Oh! long as rolls the billow,
Shall England rule the wave!

Stephen Ralph Glover was one of the most prolific composers of ballads in the nineteenth century and produced almost 1500 compositions including a chamber opera. One of his most successful songs was the duet 'What are the Wild Waves Saying?' inspired by Dickens' *Dombey and Son*. His brother Charles W. Glover earned immortality with his setting of *The Rose of Tralee*.

'The Sea is England's Glory' is in Glover's best patriotic vein. His setting of Lake's bombastic verses matches the sentiments exactly even down to the fanfares. Somehow, though, he manages to inject a melodic charm which lesser composers dispense with in the face of similar poetry.

2

HAUL THE BOWLIN'!

From the earliest recorded times, sailors have given vent to more or less musical cries to help them work together on arduous ship-board tasks. As early as the fifth century the oarsmen of a Greek galley would get under way as they echoed phrases established by a lead singer. In *The Complaynte of Scotland* (c. 1450) there is a description of a ship leaving the Firth of Forth, which includes the texts of several songs used on that occasion.

The origin of the word 'shanty' to describe a sailor's work-song may likewise be rooted in antiquity. It may be a version of the French 'chanter' or it may have found its way into naval parlance via the West Indies, where seaside huts or 'shanties' were moved away from their exposed positions with the approach of the hurricane season on great rollers hauled by teams of men. The men used to sing as they worked under the direction of a 'shantyman' perched on the ridge of each hut.

On board ship, various kinds of shanties were developed to match the effort required for different sorts of work. Thus there were halliard or hauling songs for setting the sails, windlass or capstan songs for heaving the anchor and pump songs for pumping out the ship. The rhythm of each song was dictated by the nature of the job in hand – short, sharp pulls in unison in the case of the halliards and a steady plod to heave the capstan round. One well-known type of shanty was the 'stamp-and-go' song, used, for instance, in hauling up a ship's boat when a team of men would grasp a rope and stamp away together along the deck. This was the only type of shanty allowed in the Royal Navy, and then only on less important vessels. There was also a general taboo on the singing of shanties during off-duty times. They were far too definitely associated with work.

THE DRUNKEN SAILOR

Words and Music : Traditional

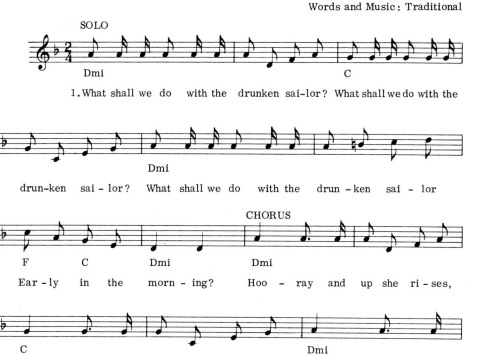

SOLO

Dmi   C

1. What shall we do with the drunken sai-lor? What shall we do with the

Dmi

drun-ken sai - lor? What shall we do with the drun - ken sai - lor

CHORUS

F   C   Dmi   Dmi

Ear - ly   in   the   morn - ing?   Hoo - ray   and   up she ri - ses,

C   Dmi

Hoo - ray   and   up she   ri - ses,   Hoo - ray   and

F   C   Dmi

up   she   ri - ses   Ear - ly   in   the   morn - ing !

THE DRUNKEN SAILOR

1. What shall we do with the drunken sailor?
   What shall we do with the drunken sailor?
   What shall we do with the drunken sailor
   Early in the morning?

CHORUS   Hooray and up she rises,
          Hooray and up she rises,
          Hooray and up she rises
          Early in the morning!

2.   Put him in the long boat 'till he's sober!
     Put him in the long boat 'till he's sober!
     Put him in the long boat 'till he's sober
     Early in the morning!

CHORUS   Hooray and up she rises,
          Hooray and up she rises,
          Hooray and up she rises
          Early in the morning!

3.   Pull out the plug and wet him all over!
     Pull out the plug and wet him all over!
     Pull out the plug and wet him all over
     Early in the morning!

CHORUS   Hooray and up she rises,
          Hooray and up she rises,
          Hooray and up she rises
          Early in the morning!

4.   Put him in the scuppers with a hose pipe on him!
     Put him in the scuppers with a hose pipe on him!
     Put him in the scuppers with a hose pipe on him
     Early in the morning!

CHORUS   Hooray and up she rises,
          Hooray and up she rises,
          Hooray and up she rises
          Early in the morning!

5.   Heave him by the leg in a running bowlin'!
     Heave him by the leg in a running bowlin'!
     Heave him by the leg in a running bowlin'
     Early in the morning!

CHORUS   Hooray and up she rises, etc.

One of the best known of all sea shanties, 'What Shall We Do With The
Drunken Sailor?' is a windlass and capstan work song. It was a favourite

runabout or 'stamp and go' shanty and, unlike many, it did not require a soloist, being originally sung by all hands as they ran away with the braces when swinging the yards round in tacking the ship.

Many versions of the song exist and its modal melody has suffered many a change. As R. R. Terry pointed out: 'I have generally found that perversions of the tune are due to sailors who took to the sea as young men in the last days of the sailing ship and consequently did not imbibe to the full the old traditions. With the intolerance of youth, they assumed that the modal turn given to a shanty by the older sailor was the mark of ignorance, since it did not square with their idea of a major or minor key.' No amount of 'regularising', however, can disguise the old modality of this popular shanty.

JOHNNY COME DOWN TO HILO

Words and Music: Traditional

SOLO

G   D   G   D

1. I neb-ber see de like since I been born, When a

G   A7   D   G   D

big buck nigger wid his sea boots on, Says "Johnny come down to Hi-lo,

CHORUS

A7   D   G   D   G   D   G   D

Poor old   man!" Oh! wake her, Oh! shake her, Oh! wake dat girl wid de

G   A7   D   G   D   A7   D

blue dress on! When Johnny comes down to Hi-lo, Poor old man!

JOHNNY COME DOWN TO HILO

1. I nebber see de like since I been born,
   When a big buck nigger wid his sea boots on,
   Says "Johnny come down to Hilo,
   Poor old man!"

CHORUS   Oh! wake her, Oh! shake her,
         Oh! wake dat girl wid de blue dress on!
         When Johnny comes down to Hilo,
         Poor old man.

2. I lub a little girl across de sea,
   She's a Badian beauty, and she says to me,

"Oh! Johnny come down to Hilo,
Poor old man!"

CHORUS   Oh! wake her, Oh! shake her, etc.

3.   Have you ebber seen de old Plantation boss
Wid de long tailed filly and de big black hoss?
When Johnny come down to Hilo,
Poor old man!

CHORUS   Oh! wake her, Oh! shake her, etc.

4.   I nebber seen de like since I been born,
When a big buck nigger wid his sea boots on,
Says "Johnny come down to Hilo,
Poor old man!"

CHORUS   Oh! wake her, Oh! shake her, etc.

One of the many purely negro shanties, 'Johnny Come Down to Hilo' is also a windlass and capstan one. The great early twentieth-century writer on the subject of the sea, Frank Bullen, has rosy memories of hearing it on 'a dewy morning in the Garden Reach where we lay just off the King of Oudh's palace awaiting our permit to moor. I was before the mast in one of Bates' ships, the *Herat*, and when the order came at dawn to man the windlass I raised this shanty and my shipmates sang the chorus as I never heard it sung before or since ... sometimes, even now, I can in fancy hear its mellow notes reverberating amid the fantastic buildings of the palace and see the great flocks of pigeons rising and falling as the strange sounds disturbed them.'

BLOW THE MAN DOWN

Words and Music : Traditional

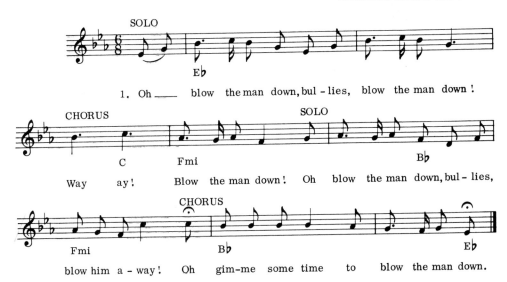

1. Oh ___ blow the man down, bul-lies, blow the man down!
Way ay! Blow the man down! Oh blow the man down, bul-lies,
blow him a-way! Oh gim-me some time to blow the man down.

BLOW THE MAN DOWN

   1.   Oh blow the man down, bullies, blow the man down!
CHORUS Way ay! Blow the man down!
         Oh blow the man down, bullies, blow him away!
CHORUS Oh gimme some time to blow the man down.

   2.   As I was a walking down Paradise Street,
CHORUS Way ay! Blow the man down!
         A saucy young damsel I happened to meet,
CHORUS Oh gimme some time to blow the man down

   3.   I says to her, "Polly, and how d'ye do?"
CHORUS Way ay! Blow the man down!
         She says, "None the better for seeing of you!"
CHORUS Oh gimme some time to blow the man down.

4. Oh we'll blow the man up and we'll blow the man down,
CHORUS Way ay! Blow the man down!
We'll blow him away into Liverpool Town,
CHORUS Oh gimme some time to blow the man down.

This halliard shanty comes from the old days of the Atlantic packet ships. Then 'blow' meant 'strike' and the song refers to the rough justice aboard at a time when the third mate was commonly called the 'third blower and striker'. References to Liverpool's 'Paradise Street' abound in shanties of the period. It must have been one of the most famous streets in all the world – sung about wherever sailors were found. The similarity between the openings of 'Blow the Man Down' and the German Christmas Carol 'Stille Nacht, Heilige Nacht' must be purely coincidental!

WHISKY JOHNNY

Words and Music: Traditional

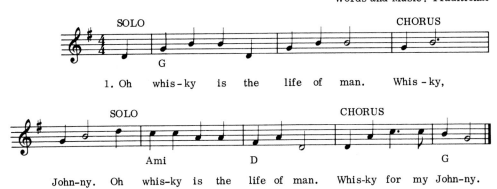

SOLO ... CHORUS

1. Oh whis-ky is the life of man. Whis-ky,

SOLO ... CHORUS

John-ny. Oh whis-ky is the life of man. Whis-ky for my John-ny.

WHISKY JOHNNY

  1. Oh whisky is the life of man.
CHORUS Whisky, Johnny.
     Oh whisky is the life of man.
CHORUS Whisky for my Johnny.

  2. Whisky makes me pawn my clothes.
CHORUS Whisky, Johnny.
     And whisky gave me this red nose.
CHORUS Whisky for my Johnny.

  3. Whisky killed my poor old dad.
CHORUS Whisky, Johnny.
     And whisky drove my mother mad.
CHORUS Whisky for my Johnny.

  4. Whisky up and whisky down.
CHORUS Whisky, Johnny.
     And whisky all around the town.
CHORUS Whisky for my Johnny.

5. Oh whisky here and whisky there.
CHORUS Whisky, Johnny.
        Oh I'll have whisky everywhere.
CHORUS Whisky for my Johnny.

6. Oh whisky is the life of man.
CHORUS Whisky, Johnny.
        Oh whisky in an old tin can.
CHORUS Whisky for my Johnny

This popular halliard shanty hymns something dear to the hearts of sailors of every age. Its lines, however, carry a dreadful warning about drinking to excess – something, surely, no sailor would do!

FIRE DOWN BELOW!

Words and Music: Traditional

SOLO

F   Bb   F   C

1. Fire in the gal - ley, fire down be - low____ It's

F F7 Bb   F C F

fetch a buck-et of wa - ter, boys, there's fire down be - low.

CHORUS

F   Bb   F   C

Fire, fire, fire down be - low, ____ It's

F F7 Bb   F C F

fetch a buck-et of wa - ter, boys, there's fire down be - low.

FIRE DOWN BELOW!

1. Fire in the galley, fire down below;
It's fetch a bucket of water, boys,
There's fire down below.

CHORUS Fire! fire! fire down below;
It's fetch a bucket of water, boys,
There's fire down below.

2. Fire in the forepeak, fire down below;
It's fetch a bucket of water, boys,
There's fire down below.

CHORUS   Fire! fire! fire down below; etc.

3.   Fire in the windlass, fire in the chain;
It's fetch a bucket of water, boys,
And put it out again.

CHORUS   Fire! fire! fire down below; etc.

4.   Fire up aloft and fire down below;
It's fetch a bucket of water, boys,
There's fire down below.

CHORUS   Fire! fire! fire down below; etc.

Originally a pumping shanty, 'Fire Down Below' survived the advent of iron and steel ships which did not need pumping by hand by rapidly turning into a capstan shanty – a purpose for which it was admirably suited. As a technical tour of a sailing ship it has endeared itself to sailors down the ages.

Fire aboard ship was certainly no joking matter. The joke in this song is that none of the sites of fire referred to were, in fact, inflammable. Of course, there was always a fire in the galley – to cook on.

HAUL AWAY, JOE

Words and Music: Traditional

HAUL AWAY, JOE

1.   Way, haul away, we'll haul away the bowlin'.
CHORUS   Way, haul away, we'll haul away, Joe.
     Way, haul away, the packet is a rollin'.
CHORUS   Way, haul away, we'll haul away, Joe.

2.   Oh, once I had an Irish girl, and she was fat and lazy.
CHORUS   Way, haul away, we'll haul away, Joe.
     Then I had a Spanish girl, she nearly drove me crazy.
CHORUS   Way, haul away, we'll haul away, Joe.

3.   When I was a little boy, and so my mother told me,
CHORUS   Way, haul away, we'll haul away, Joe
     That if I didn't kiss the girls, my lips would go all mouldy.
CHORUS   Way, haul away, we'll haul away, Joe.

4.   Way, haul away, we'll hang and haul together.
CHORUS   Way, haul away, we'll haul away, Joe.
           Way, haul away, we'll haul for better weather.
CHORUS   Way, haul away, we'll haul away, Joe.

This shanty was used to time the great collective pull on the foresheet rope. The Shantyman sang the first line, the other sailors sang the second and the haul came on the last word – 'Joe'. Irish sailors presented their own particular version of the words:

Once I was in Ireland, digging turf and 'taties
But now I'm on a lime-juice ship, hauling on the braces.

King Louis was the King of France before the Revolution,
But Louis got his head cut off, which spoiled his constitution.

Once I married an Irish girl, and her name was Flannigan,
She stole my money, she stole my clothes, she stole my plate and pannikin.

St Patrick was a gentleman, he came of dacent people,
He built a church in Dublin town and on it put a steeple.

CLEAR DE TRACK!

Words and Music: Traditional

Gmi   Dmi   Gmi   Dmi

1. Oh, de smartest pack-et you can find, Ah - ho, way-ho, are

Gmi   F

you most done? Is the Marg-'ret Ev-ans of the Blue Star line. So

Gmi   Dmi   Gmi   Bb   F

clear de track, let de bull - gine run. To me hey rig-a-jig in a

Gmi   Bb

low - backed car, Ah - ho, way - ho, are you most done? With

Gmi   F   Gmi   F   Gmi

Li - za Lee all on my knee, So clear de track, let de bull - gine run.

CLEAR DE TRACK!

1.	Oh, de smartest packet you can find,
CHORUS	Ah-ho, way-ho, are you 'most done?
	Is the Marg'ret Evans of the Blue Star Line.
CHORUS	So clear de track, let de bullgine run.

To me hey rig-a-jig in a low-backed car,

CHORUS   Ah-ho, way-ho, are you 'most done?

With Liza Lee all on my knee,

CHORUS   So clear de track, let de bullgine run.

2.   Oh, Liza Lee will you be mine?

CHORUS   Ah-ho, way-ho, are you 'most done?

I'll dress you up in silk so fine.

CHORUS   So clear de track, let de bullgine run.

To me hey rig-a-jig in a low-backed car,

CHORUS   Ah-ho, way-ho, are you 'most done?

With Liza Lee all on my knee,

CHORUS   So clear de track, let de bullgine run.

3.   And when I'm home again from sea,

CHORUS   Ah-ho, way-ho, are you 'most done?

Oh Liza, you shall marry me,

CHORUS   So clear de track, let de bullgine run.

To me hey rig-a-jig in a low-backed car,

CHORUS   Ah-ho, way-ho, are you 'most done?

With Liza Lee all on my knee,

CHORUS   So clear de track, let de bullgine run.

4.   I'll stay with you upon de shore,

CHORUS   Ah-ho, way-ho, are you 'most done?

And back to sea will go no more.

CHORUS   So clear de track, let de bullgine run.

To me hey rig-a-jig in a low-backed car,

CHORUS   Ah-ho, way-ho, are you 'most done?

With Liza Lee all on my knee,

CHORUS   So clear de track, let de bullgine run.

Negro sailors were never particular where they got their tunes from. The hymns of evangelists like Sankey and Moody were just as suitable for their purposes as music hall songs. The melody of 'Clear de Track' is quite obviously an Irish folk song – 'Shule Agra'. The reference to the 'low-backed car' is further evidence of the song's provenance. But then it was a perfect windlass shanty. (Bullgine, of course, means engine.)

HIGH BARBAREE

Words and Music : Traditional

1.There was a gal-lant Eng-lish ship a sail-ing on the sea, Blow high,____ blow low, ____ and so ___ say ____ we; And her Cap-tain he was search-ing for a pi - rate e - ne - my, Cruis-ing down a-long the coast of the High Bar - ba - ree. ____

HIGH BARBAREE

  1.   There was a gallant English ship a-sailing on the sea,
CHORUS Blow high, blow low, and so say we;
       And her Captain he was searching for a pirate enemy,
CHORUS Cruising down along the coast of the High Barbaree.

  2.   "Look ahead, look astern, look a-weather and a-lee,"
CHORUS Blow high, blow low, and so say we;
       "Aloft there at the masthead just see what you can see,"
CHORUS Cruising down along the coast of the High Barbaree.

3. "There's nought upon the stern, there's nought upon the lee,"
CHORUS   Blow high, blow low, and so say we;
"But there's a lofty ship to windward and she's sailing fast and free,
CHORUS   Cruising down along the coast of the High Barbaree."

4. "O hail her! O hail her!" our gallant Captain cried,
CHORUS   Blow high, blow low, and so say we;
"Are you a man-o-war or a privateer?" said he,
CHORUS   "Cruising down along the coast of the High Barbaree."

5. "O I am not a man-o-war nor privateer," said he;
CHORUS   Blow high, blow low, and so say we;
"But I'm a salt-sea pirate whose a-looking for his fee,
CHORUS   Cruising down along the coast of the High Barbaree."

6. O 'twas broadside to broadside a long time lay we,
CHORUS   Blow high, blow low, and so say we;
Until we shot her masts away and blew them in the sea,
CHORUS   Cruising down along the coast of the High Barbaree.

Not, strictly speaking, a shanty, 'High Barbaree' was really a forecastle song. Many versions exist but its main theme – an encounter between the English and Barbary pirates – places it roughly in the early eighteenth century while its variants suggest that it was popular enough to be altered considerably through use.

HAUL THE BOWLIN'!

Words and Music: Traditional

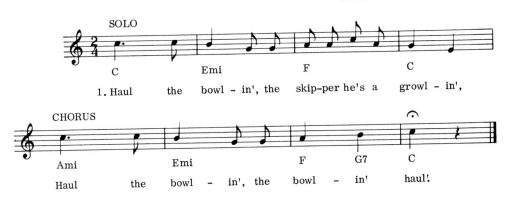

SOLO

C   Emi   F   C

1. Haul   the   bowl - in',   the   skip-per he's a   growl - in',

CHORUS

Ami   Emi   F   G7   C

Haul   the   bowl - in',   the   bowl - in'   haul!

HAUL THE BOWLIN'!

1.   Haul the bowlin', the skipper he's a-growlin',
CHORUS   Haul the bowlin', the bowlin' haul!

2.   Haul the bowlin', so early in the morning,
CHORUS   Haul the bowlin', the bowlin' haul!

3.   Haul the bowlin', the chief mate he's a-growlin'
CHORUS   Haul the bowlin', the bowlin' haul!

4.   Haul the bowlin', the wind it is a-howlin'
CHORUS   Haul the bowlin', the bowlin' haul!

5.   Haul the bowlin', the ship she is a-rollin'
CHORUS   Haul the bowlin', the bowlin' haul!

The oldest of the short-drag shanties, 'Haul on the Bowlin'' was probably popular in the reign of Henry VIII. It was certainly not used for hauling the bowline, which is a weak rope used only to extend and stop a foresail or mainsail from shaking. It was, in fact, used as a foresheet shanty.

MOBILE BAY

Words and Music: Traditional

MOBILE BAY

Was you ever down in Mobile Bay?
Johnny come and tell us and pump away,
A-screwing cotton by the day?
Johnny come and tell us and pump away,
Aye, aye, pump away,
Johnny come and tell us and pump away.

This is a negro shanty used for pumping, which, like 'Fire Down Below', made the transition to steel ships as the sailors merely substituted the word 'heave' for 'pump'.

THE RIO GRANDE

Words and Music : Traditional

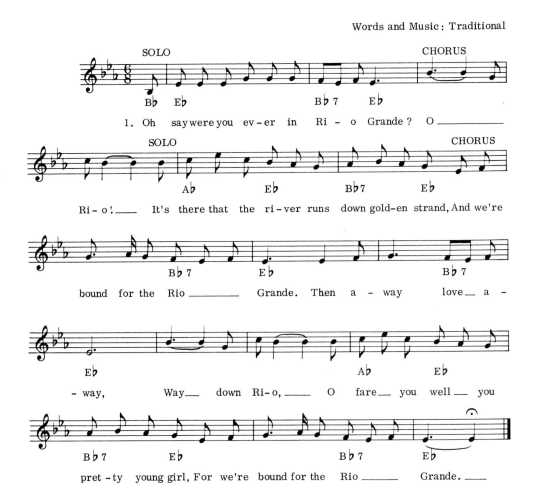

1. Oh say were you ev-er in Ri - o Grande ? O_____

Ri - o !____ It's there that the ri - ver runs down gold-en strand, And we're

bound for the Rio _____ Grande. Then a - way love_ a -

- way, Way_ down Ri - o, ____ O fare_ you well __ you

pret - ty young girl, For we're bound for the Rio _____ Grande. ____

THE RIO GRANDE

1.   O say, were you ever in Rio Grande?
CHORUS   O Rio!
      It's there that the river runs down golden strand;
CHORUS   And we're bound for the Rio Grande.

CHORUS   Then away love, away,
              Way down Rio,
              O fare you well my pretty young girl,
              For we're bound for the Rio Grande.

2.   Say goodbye to Polly and goodbye to Sue,
CHORUS   O Rio!
              And you who are listening, it's goodbye to you,
CHORUS   And we're bound for the Rio Grande.
CHORUS   Then away love, away, etc.

3.   Goodbye and farewell to you ladies of town,
CHORUS   O Rio!
              We've left you enough for to buy a silk gown,
CHORUS   And we're bound for the Rio Grande.
CHORUS   Then away love, away, etc.

4.   Now fill up your glasses and sing fare you well,
CHORUS   O Rio!
              To all the young lasses who love you so well,
CHORUS   And we're bound for the Rio Grande.
CHORUS   Then away love, away, etc.

This is, quite simply, the grandest shanty of them all. The open vowels make it eminently singable and the catchy tune has made it a firm favourite throughout the centuries. It was used on board ship as a capstan shanty but almost exclusively when hauling up the anchor at the beginning of a voyage. One authority sets the date of 'Rio Grande' at 1849, finding evidence that its popularity coincided with the Californian Gold Rush. Most writers, however, place it earlier.

SHENANDOAH

Words and Music : Traditional

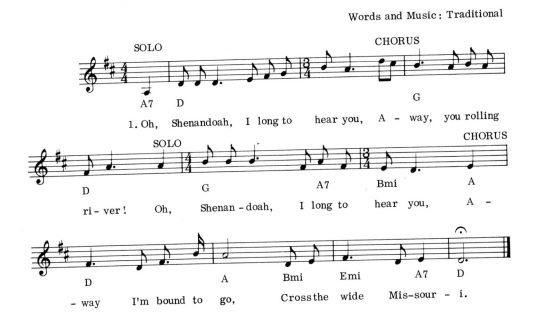

SOLO — CHORUS — A7 D G
1. Oh, Shenandoah, I long to hear you, A - way, you rolling

SOLO — CHORUS — D G A7 Bmi A
ri - ver! Oh, Shenan - doah, I long to hear you, A -

D A Bmi Emi A7 D
- way I'm bound to go, Cross the wide Mis-sour - i.

SHENANDOAH

1. Oh, Shenandoah, I long to hear you,
CHORUS Away, you rolling river!
Oh, Shenandoah, I long to hear you,
CHORUS Away I'm bound to go,
'Cross the wide Missouri.

2. Oh, Shenandoah, I love your daughter.
CHORUS Away, you rolling river!
Oh, Shenandoah, I love your daughter.
CHORUS Away I'm bound to go,
'Cross the wide Missouri.

3. Oh, Shenandoah, I took a notion,
CHORUS Away, you rolling river!

To sail across the stormy ocean.
CHORUS Away I'm bound to go,
'Cross the wide Missouri.

4. Oh, Shenandoah, I'm bound to leave you.
CHORUS Away, you rolling river!
Oh, Shenandoah, I'll not deceive you.
CHORUS Away I'm bound to go,
'Cross the wide Missouri.

One of the most popular of all shanties, 'Shenandoah' came from the southern states of America and tells the story of an American's wooing of the daughter of the legendary Indian Chief, Shenandoah, after whom many towns in the United States have been named. As a shanty it was used as a windlass or capstan work song.

3

STAND TO YOUR GUNS!

Merely to keep a ship at sea in the days of sail required a degree of skill and hard labour which, today, is hard to conceive; the fact that a ship was often used in addition as a fighting platform almost defies belief. And yet for centuries, armed with varying numbers of guns, sailing ships did battle with each other on the high seas with results that were often decisive for the nations they represented.

A man-o'-war has always required a much larger crew than a merchant ship of comparable size, and in times of war nations have often had to compel men to join the fleet in sufficient numbers. Once at sea they would find themselves under harsh discipline – silence rather than song was the rule as they went about their business – and they lived in ludicrously cramped conditions below decks. The life of each mess was centred literally on the gun manned by its members; they ate by the side of it, slung their hammocks above it, cleared the decks to allow for its recoil in action and in many cases died by it, if an enemy broadside should rake the deck on which they worked. And death indeed must sometimes have seemed preferable to the rough treatment given to the wounded by the surgeons, whose readiness for the fray must have been one of the most ominous signs of an approaching action.

Scenes of horror, then, but scenes of heroism too, and the song makers chose to concentrate on that aspect of the fighting sailor's life. But one can't help wondering how some poor old wreck of a former gunner's mate would have reacted to the sentiments of 'Stand to Your Guns!'

THE SAUCY ARETHUSA

Written by PRINCE HOARE

Composed by WILLIAM SHIELD

Allegro con spirito

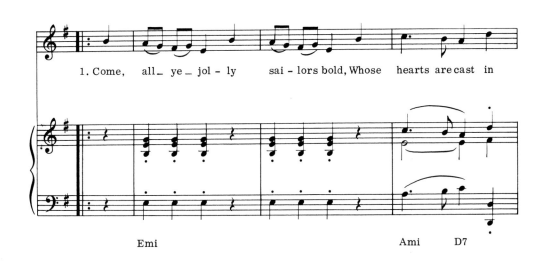

1. Come, all ye jol - ly sai - lors bold, Whose hearts are cast in

Emi   Ami   D7

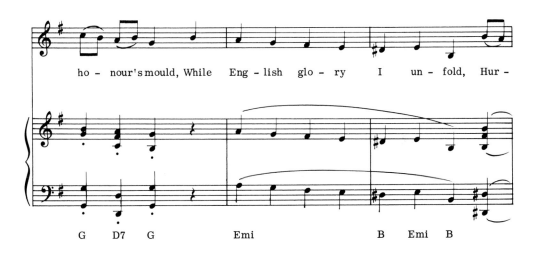

ho - nour's mould, While Eng - lish glo - ry I un - fold, Hur -

G   D7   G   Emi   B   Emi   B

Soon-er than strike we'll all ex-pire, On board of the A-re-thu-sa.

Emi B Emi Ami B

Emi

THE SAUCY ARETHUSA

1. Come, all you jolly sailors bold,
   Whose hearts are cast in honour's mould,
   While English glory I unfold,
   Hurrah for the Arethusa!
   She is a frigate tight and brave,
   As ever stemm'd the dashing wave,
   Her men are staunch to their fav'rite launch,
   And when the foe shall meet our fire,
   Sooner than strike we'll all expire,
   On board of the Arethusa.

2. 'Twas with the spring fleet she went out,
   The English Channel to cruise about,
   When four French sail, in show so stout,
   Bore down on the Arethusa.

The fam'd *Belle Poule* straight ahead did lie,
The Arethusa seem'd to fly,
Not a sheet, or a tack, or a brace did she slack,
Tho' the Frenchmen laugh'd, and thought it stuff,
But they knew not the handful of men, so tough,
On board of the Arethusa.

3. On deck five hundred men did dance,
   The stoutest they could find in France;
   We with two hundred did advance
   On board of the Arethusa.
   The Captain hail'd the Frenchman, "Ho!"
   The Frenchman then cried out "Hallo!"
   "Bear down, d'ye see, to our Admiral's lee,"
   "No, no," says the Frenchman, "that can't be,"
   "Then I must lug you along with me",
   Says the saucy Arethusa.

4. The fight was off the Frenchman's land,
   We drove them back up on their strand,
   For we fought till not a stick would stand
   Of the gallant Arethusa.
   And now we've driven the foe ashore,
   Never to fight with Britons more,
   Let each fill a glass to his fav'rite lass!
   A health to the captain and officers true,
   And all that belong to the jovial crew
   On board of the Arethusa.

In William Shield's musical play *Lock and Key*, produced at Covent Garden in 1796, the hero, a naval officer, sang 'The Saucy Arethusa' under the window of his lady-love. Although hardly the most appropriate serenade the song achieved immediate and lasting popularity. Shield (1748–1829) has been described as the most English composer since Purcell and certainly his output of songs, panto-mimes, operas and musical plays reflect that lyricism and skill in word-setting with which Purcell is so much associated. Shield was made Master of the King's Musick in 1817.

The words of the song were written by the artist and author Prince Hoare whose other works include the well-known opera by Stephen Storace – 'No Song No Supper'.

The adventure of the *Arethusa* to which the song refers was not in fact quite so 'hurrah provoking' as Hoare suggests. She gave chase to and engaged the French ship *La Belle Poule* in June 1778. The Frenchman directed his fire chiefly at the *Arethusa*'s rigging and spars, disabled her and made off leaving the English ship to be towed back to the fleet. Casualties on the French side were certainly heavier but then the *Arethusa* was a slightly stronger ship. Hard facts, however, seldom make for good lyrics and Prince Hoare wisely avoided them. Eight months after this engagement the *Arethusa* was wrecked at sea whilst pursuing the enemy.

THE GOLDEN VANITY

Words and music : Traditional [arr.A.M.]

1.O I have a ship in the North Coun-try, And she goes __ by the name __ of the Gol - den Va - ni-ty, And I fear she will be ta - ken by some Tur- kish Ga - li - lee As she

THE GOLDEN VANITY

1. O I have a ship in the North Country,
    And she goes by the name of the Golden Vanity,
    And I fear she will be taken by some Turkish galilee
    As she sails along the Lowlands low.

CHORUS   Lowlands, Lowlands, as she sails along the Lowlands low.

2. To the Captain then upspake the little cabin boy,
    He said: 'What will you give me if the galley I destroy –
    The Turkish galilee, if no more it shall annoy,
    As we sail in the Lowlands low?''

CHORUS   Lowlands, Lowlands, etc.

3.   "Of silver and gold I will give you a store;
     And my pretty little daughter that lives on the shore,
     Of treasure and of fee as well, I'll give thee galore,
     As we sail along the Lowlands low."

CHORUS   Lowlands, Lowlands, etc.

4.   The boy bared his breast and straightaway leapt in,
     And he held in his hand an auger sharp and thin,
     And he swam until he came to the Turkish galleon,
     As she lay in the Lowlands low.

CHORUS   Lowlands, Lowlands, etc.

5.   And some were playing cards and some were playing dice,
     He bored three holes once and he bored three holes twice.
     The water all flowed in and it dazzled in their eyes,
     As she sank in the Lowlands low.

CHORUS   Lowlands, Lowlands, etc.

6.   Then the cabin boy swam round to the starboard side,
     Saying "Messmates, take me up, for I'm drifting with the tide."
     And they laid him on the deck and he closed his eyes and died
     As they sailed in the Lowlands low.

CHORUS   Lowlands, Lowlands, etc.

The date of this ballad is uncertain but it is thought to be about 1635. At that time the Barbary pirates were at the height of their power in the Mediterranean and a great threat to shipping. Many versions of the melody exist but there are surprisingly few variants of the words of this song – although it often appears under its alternative title – 'Lowlands Low'. As long as people enjoy a good rousing chorus 'The Golden Vanity' is assured of its popularity.

POOR JOE, THE MARINE

Written and composed by JOHN ASHLEY

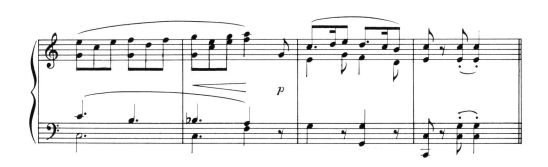

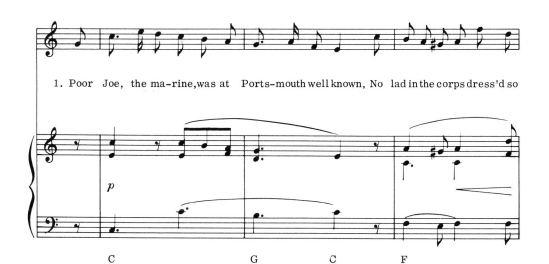

1. Poor Joe, the ma-rine, was at Ports-mouth well known, No lad in the corps dress'd so

POOR JOE, THE MARINE

1. Poor Joe, the marine, was at Portsmouth well known,
   No lad in the corps dress'd so smart;
   The lasses ne'er looked at the lad with a frown,
   His manliness won every heart.
   Sweet Polly at Portsmouth he took for his bride,
   And surely there never was seen
   A couple so gay march to church, side by side,
   As Polly and Joe the marine.

2. The bright torch of Hymen was scarce in a blaze,
   When thundering drums they heard rattle;
   And Joe in an instant was forc'd to the seas
   To give a bold enemy battle.
   The action was dreadful, each ship a mere wreck,
   Such slaughter few sailors have seen;
   Two hundred brave fellows lay strew'd on the deck,
   And among them poor Joe the marine.

3. But victory - faithful to brave British tars,
   At length put an end to the fight;
   Then homeward they steer'd, full of glory and scars,
   And soon had fam'd Portsmouth in sight.
   The ramparts were crowded, the heroes to greet,
   And foremost sweet Polly was seen;
   But the very first sailor she chanc'd for to meet,
   Told the fate of poor Joe the marine.

The fate of too many young sailors is commemorated in this song by John
Ashley. But it is typical of the type of sea ballad that was immensely popular
between about 1780 and 1830 when Charles Dibdin was writing. The easy
melodic style had great appeal and 'Poor Joe the Marine' has lost none of its
charm.

John or Josiah Ashley (1780-1830) lived most of his life in Bath where he
taught music and sang in concerts. He wrote many songs and ballads which
were highly successful. He also wrote two pamphlets on the origins of the
English National Anthem - a subject that was being hotly debated in the late
1820s.

STAND TO YOUR GUNS!

Written and composed by THOMAS CARTER

Stand to your guns! my hearts of oak, Let not a word on

Ram home your guns and sponge them well, Let us be sure the

balls will tell, The can-non's roar shall sound their knell,

Ram home your guns and sponge them well, Let us be sure the

balls will tell, The can-non's roar shall sound their knell; Be stea - dy, be

stea - dy, be stea-dy, boys, be stea-dy.   Be stea - dy,

be stea - dy,   Be stea - dy, boys, be

stea-dy,   Be stea - dy, boys, be stea-dy, Be   stea - dy, boys, be

stea – dy.

Not yet, nor yet, nor yet; ___ Re – serve your fire, I

do de – sire, Not yet, nor yet, nor yet, Not yet, nor yet, nor

yet, Re – serve your fire, I do de – sire, Not yet, nor yet, nor

Gods a-maz'd be - hold the — bat-tle, the bat-tle, the bat-tle, the

bat-tle, the bat - tle, the bat - tle, the bat-tle. A

broad - side, my boys.

A broad - side, my boys!

fly, Con-quer, boys, or brave-ly die, or brave-ly

die, or brave-ly die! Hurl des-truc-tion on your

foes, Hurl des-truc-tion on your foes. She___

sinks, she sinks, she sinks, Huz-za! She sinks, she sinks, she

STAND TO YOUR GUNS!

Stand to your guns! my hearts of oak,
Let not a word on board be spoke,
Victory soon will crown the joke;
Be silent and be ready.

Ram home your guns and sponge them well,
Let us be sure ... the balls will tell,
The cannon's roar shall sound their knell,
Be steady, boys, be steady.

Not yet, nor yet, nor yet ...
Reserve your fire, I do desire,
Fire!

Now, the elements do rattle,
The Gods amaz'd behold the battle –
A broadside, my boys.

See the blood in purple tide,
Trickle down her batter'd side,
Wing'd with fate the bullets fly,
Conquer, boys, or bravely die!

Hurl destruction on your foes!
She sinks, Huzza! to the bottom,
To the bottom down she goes!

Thomas Carter, the composer of this song, was born in Ireland in the second half of the eighteenth century and died in London in 1804 having written scores of songs and several musical dramas. His most famous song – 'Nannie, wilt thou gang wi' me' – achieved an enormous success and earned him a reputation probably far in excess of his true worth as a composer. He did, however, have the knack of turning out a jolly good tune when one was needed. The hymn tune 'Helmsley' – now sung to the words 'Lo, He comes with clouds descending' – was adapted from one of his ballads entitled 'Guardian Angels'. We have included his song 'Stand to your Guns' partly because it enjoyed enormous popularity in the early nineteenth century when similar dramatic pieces were very much in vogue but also because the singer who attempts Braham's 'Death of Nelson' (page 129) may well need an encore.

Something, perhaps, should be said on behalf of Carter as a poet. It is doubtful, however, whether it ever will be.

WILL WATCH

Written and composed by JOHN DAVY

Moderato

1. One   morn when the   wind from the

north-ward blew_ keen-ly, While sul - len-ly   roar'd the big   waves of_ the_

shore;__ When his pock - ets__ were __ lin'd, Why his life should be mend - ed, The laws he had bro - ken he'd__ ne - ver break more.

WILL WATCH

1. One morn when the wind from the northward blew keenly,
   While sullenly rear'd the big waves of the main,
   A fam'd smuggler, Will Watch, kiss'd his Sue, then serenely
   Took helm, and to sea boldly steer'd out again.

Will had promis'd his Sue that his trip, if well ended,
Should coil up his hopes and he'd anchor on shore;
When his pockets were lin'd, why his life should be mended,
The laws he had broken he'd never break more.

2.   His sea boat was trim, made her port, took her lading;
Then Will stood for home, reach'd the offing, and cried,
"This night, if I've luck, furls the sail of my trading;
In dock I can lie, serve a friend, too, beside."
Will lay-to till night came on, darksome and dreary;
To crowd ev'ry sail, then, he pip'd up each hand;
But a signal soon 'spied – 'twas a prospect uncheery –
A signal that warn'd them to steer from the land.

3.   "The Philistines are out!" cries Will – "we'll take no heed on't;
Attack'd, whose the man who will flinch from his gun?
Should my head be blown off, I shall ne'er feel the need on't
We'll fight while we can; when we can't, boys, we'll run."
Through the haze of the night, a bright flash now appearing,
"Oh, oh!" cries Will Watch, "the Philistines bear down;
Bear a hand, my tight lads, ere we think about sheering –
One broadside pour in, should we swim, boys, or drown.

4.   But should I be popp'd off, you, my mates, left behind me,
Regard my last words, see 'em kindly obey'd;
Let no stone mark the spot; and, my friends, do you mind me,
Near the beach is the grave where Will Watch would be laid."
Poor Will's yarn was spun out – for a bullet next minute
Laid him low on the deck, and he never spoke more:
His bold crew fought the brig while a shot remain'd in it,
Then sheer'd off and Will's hulk to his Susan they bore.

5.   In the dead of the night his last wish was complied with,
To few known his grave, and to few known his end:
He was borne to the earth by the crew that he died with,
He'd the tears of his Susan, the prayers of each friend.
Near his grave dash the billows, the winds loudly bellow:
Yon ash, struck with lightning, points out the cold bed
Where Will Watch, the bold smuggler, that fam'd lawless fellow,
Once fear'd, now forgot, sleeps in peace with the dead.

John Davy (1765-1824), the composer of 'Will Watch', was born in Upton-Helion near Exeter, came to London in his thirties and earned his living as a composer and teacher. As a very young child he showed immense musical precocity allied to kleptomania. At the age of six he stole between twenty and thirty horseshoes from a neighbouring smithy, selected the ones that would make a complete octave, hung them up in an upper room and imitated the chimes of the church bells in nearby Crediton. As a composer he is chiefly remembered for 'The Bay of Biscay' (page 214). His easy melodic style is clearly shown in this song subtitled 'The Death of the Smuggler'.

THE INVINCIBLE ARMADO

Written by JOHN O'KEEFE

Composed by SAMUEL ARNOLD

1. In May, fif-teen hun-dred and eigh-ty and eight, Cries

Phi-lip, "The Eng-lish I'll hum-ble, I've ta-ken it in-to my

ma - jes-ty's pate, And the li - on, Oh! down he shall tum - ble.

Down, down, And the li - on, Oh! down he shall

tum - ble. The

Lords of the sea!" then his scep-tre he shook, "I'll prove it all ar - rant bra-

-va - do.   By   Nep - tune I'll sweep 'em all   in - to a   nook, With th'in-

-vin-ci-ble Spa - nish Ar - ma - do.   I'll   sweep 'em all   in - to a

nook,   With th'in - vin - ci - ble Spa - nish Ar - ma - do."

THE INVINCIBLE ARMADO

1. In May, fifteen hundred and eighty and eight,
    Cries Philip, "The English I'll humble,
    I've taken it into my majesty's pate,
    And the lion, Oh! down he shall tumble.
    The Lords of the sea!" – then his sceptre he shook,
    "I'll prove it all arrant bravado.
    By Neptune I'll sweep 'em all into a nook,
    With th'invincible Spanish Armado."

2. This fleet started out and the winds they did blow;
    Their guns made a terrible clatter.
    Our noble Queen Bess, 'cos she wanted to know;
    Quill'd her ruff and cried, "Pray, what's the matter?"
    "They say, my good Queen," replies Howard so stout,
    "The Spaniard has drawn his Toledo.
    Odds bobbins! he'll thump us, and kick us about,
    With th'invincible Spanish Armado."

3. The Lord Mayor of London, a very wise man,
    What to do in the case, vastly wondered.
    Says the Queen, "Send in fifty good ships, if you can,"
    Says my Lord May'r, "I'll send you a hundred."
    Our fine ships soon struck ev'ry cannon all dumb,
    For the Dons ran to *Ave* and *Credo*.
    Don Medina roars out, "Sure the foul fiend is come
    For th'invincible Spanish Armado."

4. On Effingham's squadron, tho' all in a breast,
    Like open-mouth'd curs they came bowling.
    His sugar-plums finding they could not digest,
    Away they ran yelping, and howling.
    Whene'er Briton's foe shall, with envy agog,
    In our channel make such a tornado
    Huzza! my brave boys! we're still lusty to flog
    An Invincible Spanish Armado.

The composer of this spirited song was one of the most distinguished musicians in eighteenth-century England. Dr Samuel Arnold was organist and composer to the Chapel Royal, conductor of the Academy of Antient Musick and the editor of the first uniform edition of the works of George Frederick Handel. As well as all this, he found time to compose the music for several plays and operas which were given at Covent Garden. 'The Invincible Armado' comes from one of his musical plays – *The Siege of Cuzzola* – which was first performed in 1785. Although not as successful as some of his pieces, the songs contained in the play were published and performed frequently in the London pleasure gardens. Material success must have appealed to Dr Arnold, but one gets the impression that his mind was mainly on higher things. He died of a fall from his library steps in October 1802.

John O'Keefe (1747–1833) was an actor and dramatist whose comic plays enjoyed enormous popularity at the Haymarket and Covent Garden. Nowadays he is best remembered for the song 'I am a Friar of Orders Grey' which was featured in his *Merry Sherwood*.

THE CONSTITUTION AND THE GUERRIERE

Words and music: Traditional [arr. A. M.]

1. It of-times has been told __ How the Brit-ish sea-men bold __ Could __ flog the tars of France so neat and han - dy oh! But they ne - ver found their

THE CONSTITUTION AND THE GUERRIERE

1. It oftimes has been told
   How the British seamen bold
   Could flog the tars of France so neat and handy oh!
   But they never found their match
   Till the Yankees did them catch,
   Oh, the Yankee boys for fighting are the dandy oh!

2. The *Guerriere* so bold
   On the foaming ocean roll'd,

Commanded by proud Dacres the grandee, oh!
With as choice a British crew
As a rammer ever drew,
Could flog the Frenchmen two to one so handy, oh!

3.   When this frigate hove in view,
Says proud Dacres to his crew,
"Come, clear ship for action and be handy, oh!
On the weather gage, boys, get her,"
And to make his men fight better,
He gave to them gunpowder mixed with brandy, oh!

4.   Then Dacres loudly cries,
"Make this Yankee ship your prize,
You can in thirty minutes neat and handy, oh!
Twenty-five's enough I'm sure,
And if you'll do it in a score,
I'll treat you to a double share of brandy, oh!"

5.   The British shot flew hot,
Which the Yankees answered not,
Till they got within the distance they called handy, oh!
"Now," says Hull unto his crew,
"Boys, let's see what we can do,
If we take this boasting Briton we're the dandy, oh!"

6.   The first broadside we poured
Took her mainmast by the board,
Which made this lofty frigate look abandon'd, oh!
Then Dacres shook his head;
To his officers he said,
"Lord! I didn't think those Yankees were so handy, oh!"

7.   Our second told so well
That their fore and mizzen fell
Which dous'd the royal ensign neat and handy, oh!
"By George!" says he, "We're done,"
And they fired a lee gun,
While the Yankees struck up Yankee doodle dandy, oh!

8.   Then Dacres came on board
To deliver up his sword,

> Which he was loath to lose, it was so handy, oh!
> "Oh, keep your sword," says Hull,
> "For it only makes you dull;
> Cheer up and let us have a little brandy, oh!"

9.   Now, fill your glasses full,
> And we'll drink to Captain Hull,
> And merrily we'll push about the brandy, oh!
> John Bull may boast his fill,
> But let the world say what it will,
> The Yankee boys for fighting are the dandy, oh!

The story of how the US frigate *Constitution* took the British *Guerrière* was a favourite forecastle ballad in American ships. The words are sung to the tune of 'The Pretty Girl of Derby O!' The British had a musical revenge as well as a naval one. When the *Shannon* beat the US *Chesapeake* the same tune was given new words:

> Now the *Chesapeake* so bold
> Sail'd from Boston I've been told
> For to take a British frigate neat and handy-o.
> The people in the port
> All came out to see the sport,
> And the bands were playing 'Yankee Doodle Dandy-O!'

The song goes on to describe the British victory.

BENBOW,
THE BROTHER TAR'S SONG

Words and music : Traditional

Boldly

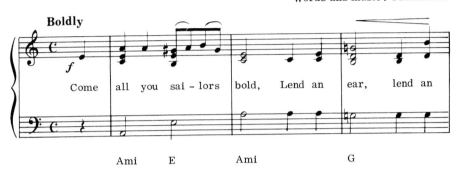

Come all you sai - lors bold, Lend an ear, lend an

Ami   E   Ami   G

ear, Come, all you sai - lors bold, lend an ear;

Dmi   E   Ami   E   Ami

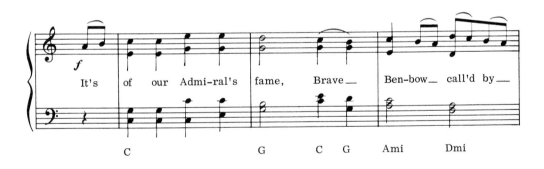

It's of our Admi-ral's fame, Brave ___ Ben-bow ___ call'd by ___

C   G   C   G   Ami   Dmi

name, How he fought on the main ___ You shall ___

E   Ami   Dmi   Ami   E

BENBOW, THE BROTHER TAR'S SONG

1. Come, all you sailors bold,
    Lend an ear, lend an ear,
    Come all you sailors bold, lend an ear;
    It's of our Admiral's fame,
    Brave Benbow call'd by name,
    How he fought on the main
    You shall hear.

2. Brave Benbow he set sail
    For to fight, for to fight,
    Brave Benbow he set sail for to fight;
    Brave Benbow he set sail,
    With a fine and pleasant gale,
    But his captains they turn'd tail
    In a fright.

3. Says Kirby unto Wade,
    "I will run, I will run,"
    Says Kirby unto Wade, "I will run:"
    I value not disgrace,
    Nor the losing of my place,
    My enemies I'll not face
    With a gun."

4. 'Twas the *Ruby* and *Noah's Ark*
    Fought the French, fought the French,
    'Twas the *Ruby* and *Noah's Ark* fought the French:
    And there was ten in all,
    Poor souls they fought them all,
    They valued them not at all,
    Nor their noise.

5. It was our Admiral's lot
    With a chain shot, with a chain shot,
    It was our Admiral's lot with a chain shot.
    Our Admiral lost his legs,
    And to his men he begs,
    "Fight on, my boys," he says,
    "'Tis my lot."

6. While the surgeon dress'd his wounds,
    Thus he said, thus he said,
    While the surgeon dress'd his wounds, thus he said:
    "Let my cradle now in haste
    On the quarter-deck be plac'd,
    That my enemies I may face
    Till I'm dead."

7. And there bold Benbow lay
    Crying out, crying out,
    And there bold Benbow lay, crying out:
    "Let us tack about once more,
    We'll drive them to their own shore,
    I value not half a score,
    Nor their noise."

Vice-Admiral John Benbow (1653–1752) was much loved by ordinary sailors because he had risen from the ranks – hence his nickname – 'The Brother Tar'. This broadside ballad telling the story of his death appeared in the second half of the eighteenth century and was as popular as the Admiral himself had been.

BRITONS, STRIKE HOME!

Written by BEAUMONT and FLETCHER

Composed by HENRY PURCELL

BRITONS, STRIKE HOME!

Britons, strike home! revenge your country's wrongs!
Fight! and record yourselves in Druids' songs!

This song which was rendered even more often than 'Heart of Oak' when ships of the Royal Navy went into battle, first appeared in a tragedy, *Bonduca* (1695) for which Henry Purcell wrote the incidental music. It was composed as a solo for the 'Chief Druid'. Later, a touching reference to the song is to be found in 'A faithfull narrative of the cruel sufferings of Captain Death and his crew' by Samuel Stoakes (1757). We read that, in the course of a terrible sea-fight, 'the Master at Arms had one of his arms and part of his body torn away: in this bloody condition he was carried down to the surgeon ... and the poor man finding himself dying, bravely in his last moments sang the song of "Britons, Strike Home" and expired with the words in his mouth.'

THE DEATH OF NELSON

Written by S. J. ARNOLD

Composed by JOHN BRAHAM

RECITATIVE

O'er Nelson's

tomb, with si - lent grief op - prest, Bri - tan - nia mourns her

he - ro! now at rest: But those bright lau - rels will not fade with

years, Whose leaves are water'd by a na - tion's tears.

Allegro maestoso

ARIA

1. 'Twas— in Tra-fal-gar's Bay We saw the foe - men lay;
2. And— now the can-non's roar A - long th'af-fright-ed shore,

Each heart was— bound - ing— then; We—
Our— Nel - son— led the — way; His —

thought of home — or beauty. A - long the line the sig-nal ran,
Eng - land, home and beauty. He cried, as 'midst the fire he ran,

cresc.

f ff

"Eng - land ex - pects that ev - 'ry — man This

f

day will — do his — du-ty, This day will —

do his — du - ty."

mf

Slower

3. At last the fa - tal wound, Which spread dis - may a -

- round,   The he - ro's   breast,   the _____

he - ro's breast re - ceiv'd,   "Heav'n fights up - on our

side! The day's our own," he cried!

Tempo I

"Now— long e - nough I've— liv'd! In ho - nour's cause my

mf

life was pass'd, In ho - nour's cause I fall at last, For

slentando

p colla voce

Eng - land, home,— and beauty, For— Eng - land, home,— and

p e legato

beauty." Thus end-ing life as he be-gan, Eng-land con-

- fess'd that ev - 'ry___ man That day had_done his_

du -ty, That day had ___ done his ___ du -ty.

THE DEATH OF NELSON

RECITATIVE O'er Nelson's Tomb, with silent grief oppress'd,
Britannia mourns her Hero, now at rest:
But those bright laurels ne'er shall fade with years,
Whose leaves are water'd by a Nation's tears.

ARIA 'Twas in Trafalgar's bay
We saw the Frenchman lay,
Each heart was bounding then.
We scorned the foreign yoke,
For our Ships were British Oak,
And hearts of oak our men!
Our Nelson mark'd them on the wave,
Three cheers our gallant Seamen gave,
Nor thought of home or beauty.
Along the line this signal ran,
England expects that ev'ry man
This day will do his duty!

And now the cannons roar
Along th'affrighted shore,
Our Nelson led the way,
His Ship the Vict'ry nam'd!
Long be that Vict'ry famed,
For Vict'ry crowned the day!
But dearly was that conquest bought,
Too well the gallant Hero fought,
For England, home and beauty.
He cried as 'midst the fire he ran,
"England shall find that ev'ry man
This day will do his duty!"

At last the fatal wound,
Which spread dismay around,
The Hero's breast received;
"Heav'n fights on our side,
The day's our own," he cried!
"Now long enough I've lived!
In honour's cause my life was past,
In honour's cause I fell at last,
For England, home and beauty."

> Thus ending life as he began,
> England confessed that ev'ry man,
> That day had done his duty!

This song was a great exhibition piece for Victorian tenors. 'The Death of Nelson' came originally from an opera by John Braham, *The Americans* which was first produced in 1811. So overcome was Lady Hamilton, who was in a private box for the evening, that she had to be taken out of the performance in a fit of hysterics. Critics have suggested that her reaction was more to the musical setting than to the words. It is really rather unimpressive – a collection of half-digested musical clichés that say more about the composer's patriotism than his musical capabilities. When all is said, however, 'The Death of Nelson' is a fine vehicle for a dramatic tenor.

The composer, John Braham (1774–1856) was well known as a tenor being reckoned by at least one writer as 'the greatest English tenor ever known'. Of Jewish origin (his real name was Abraham) he had a keen sense of business as well as of music. He sang in opera all over Europe winning acclaim from, amongst others, Napoleon. Presumably he never sang this song to the Emperor.

4

THE LASS
THAT LOVES A SAILOR

Price One Shilling Coloured

'Now all you ladies, bear in mind
A sailor's love is hard to find.
But when you've found one good and true,
Don't change the old love for the new.'

The sailor always seems to have been attractive, if unreliable, as a lover. He has about him the glamour of faraway places, he tells a good yarn, he's open handed with his money in the brief time he's ashore, and, if he wears a uniform, it is often physically flattering. Many a lower-deck sailor in the Royal Navy has been reluctant to advance to the 'fore and aft' rig of the Petty Officer because it doesn't have quite the appeal of his wide, blue-serge collar. As for the sailor's reputation of having a wife in every port, it is part of the breezy opportunism which belongs to the sailor's life: here today, gone tomorrow – shut up, maybe for months at a time, in an all-male floating prison. Though occasionally women did follow their menfolk to sea. The Captain's wife might make a voyage now and then, in which case the men had censored versions of their shanties and foc'sle ditties available, and sometimes more lightly attached ladies would be smuggled on board, some of them producing infants who merited the appellation 'son of a gun'.

As a general rule, separation was the lot of the lass who loved a sailor, and many a lyric reminds us of her longing: 'Blow the Wind Southerly' is one of the most moving examples. Jack, too, for all that roving eye of his, has always been apt to carry a memento or photograph of one special person close to him, a symbol perhaps of the permanence he lacks; and just as those on shore tend to idealise the sailor, so he, for his part, is inclined to place his chosen sweetheart on a pedestal of dreams. Whether she can maintain that position in reality depends on the luck of the draw. She may be as constant as he is; on the other hand, she may, like 'Scornful Sue', give him cause for complaint.

THE LASS THAT LOVES A SAILOR

Written and composed by CHARLES DIBDIN

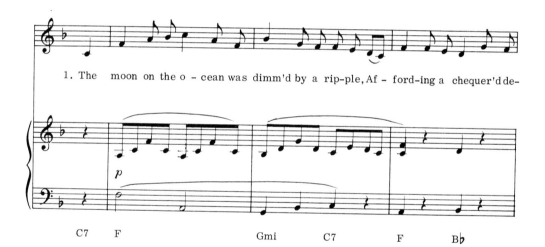

1. The moon on the o - cean was dimm'd by a rip-ple, Af - ford-ing a chequer'd de-

C7   F   Gmi   C7   F   B♭

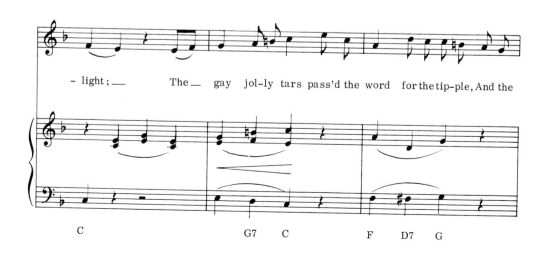

- light; ___   The ___ gay jol-ly tars pass'd the word for the tip-ple, And the

C   G7   C   F   D7   G

THE LASS THAT LOVES A SAILOR

1. The moon on the ocean was dimm'd by a ripple,
    Affording a chequer'd delight;
    The gay jolly tars pass'd the word for the tipple,
    And the toast, for 'twas Saturday night.
    Some sweetheart or wife, he lov'd as his life,
    Each drank and wish'd he could hail her;
    But the standing toast, that pleased the most,
    Was "The wind that blows, the ship that goes,
    And the lass that loves a sailor."

2. Some drank "The Queen" and some "Her brave ships",
    And some "The Constitution";
    Some "May our foes and all such rips
    Yield to English resolution";
    The fate that might bless some Poll or Bess,
    And that they soon might hail her;
    But the standing toast, that pleased the most,
    Was "The wind that blows, the ship that goes,
    And the lass that loves a sailor."

3. Some drank "The Prince" and some "Our Land",
    This glorious land of freedom;
    Some "That our tars may never want
    Heroes brave to lead them";
    "That she who's in distress may find
    Such friends as ne'er may fail her";
    But the standing toast, that pleased the most,
    Was "The wind that blows, the ship that goes,
    And the lass that loves a sailor."

Charles Dibdin's last theatrical venture was a piece put on at the Haymarket in 1811 called *The Round Robin*. It was, sadly, a disastrous failure despite the fact that it contained one of his best songs – 'The Lass that Loves a Sailor'. It is typical of the composer that he managed to compose such a melodious and lighthearted song when he himself was in bad health and ruinous financial difficulties.

Life was never easy for this giant of the sea song. Charles Dibdin was born in 1745, the twelfth of fourteen children. His father was a silversmith and his mother, the daughter of a West Country parson. Educated at Winchester where he learned the rudiments of organ playing and harmony, he travelled to London when still in his teens and with the help of his elder brother Tom (see 'Tom Bowling', page 223) became apprenticed to a music shop proprietor in Cheapside. Seeing no future in it, however, Dibdin soon devoted his life to itinerant music-making and the composition of songs. Many of these were first heard at his own 'Table Entertainments' – evenings of songs and recitations he gave himself, which were characterised by his informal and unstagey approach.

Dibdin was also very much involved in the theatre and wrote over 200 plays with music. It is, though, as a composer of sea songs that he will be best remembered. The British Government granted him a pension of £200 a year in recognition of his services, through song, to the navy. He died in 1814.

BOBBY SHAFTOE

Words and music: Traditional [arr.A.M.]

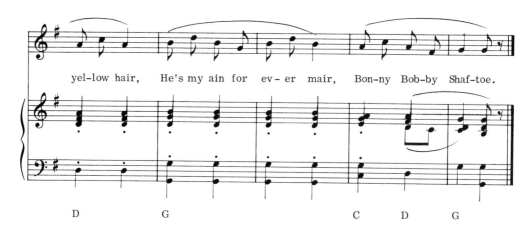

yel-low hair,   He's my ain for ev-er mair,   Bon-ny Bob-by Shaf-toe.

D   G   C   D   G

BOBBY SHAFTOE

1.   Bobby Shaftoe's gone to sea,
      Silver buckles at his knee;
      He'll come back and marry me,
      Bonny Bobby Shaftoe.
CHORUS   Bobby Shaftoe's bright and fair,
      Combing down his yellow hair,
      He's my ain for ever mair,
      Bonny Bobby Shaftoe.

2.   Bobby Shaftoe's tall and slim,
      He's always dressed so neat and trim,
      The lassies they all keek at him,
      Bonny Bobby Shaftoe.
CHORUS   Bobby Shaftoe's bright and fair,
      Combing down his yellow hair,
      He's my ain for ever mair,
      Bonny Bobby Shaftoe.

3.   Bobby Shaftoe's gett'n a bairn,
      For to dandle on his airm,
      On his airm and on his knee,
      Bobby Shaftoe loves me.
CHORUS   Bobby Shaftoe's bright and fair,
      Combing down his yellow hair,
      He's my ain for ever mair,
      Bonny Bobby Shaftoe.

Like 'Blow the Wind Southerly' (page 171) and 'When the Boat Comes in' (page 252), 'Bobby Shaftoe' is a Northumbrian folk song which has become well known far beyond that county's borders.

Folklorists have noted that in performance the hero's name is invariably pronounced 'Shafty'.

NANCY LEE

Written by FRED E. WEATHERLY   Composed by STEPHEN ADAMS

1. Of all ___ the wives as e'er you know, ___

Yeo ho! ___ lads! ho! Yeo ho! ___ yeo ___ ho! There's none ___ like Nan - cy Lee, I trow, ___

ho!— lads!— ho!— Yeo ho! The — sail - or's

D   A7   D   G

wife the sail-or's star— shall be. Yeo ho!— we — go a-

D7

-cross— the — sea,— The sail - or's wife the sail-or's star— shall

G

be, The sail-or's wife his star — shall — be. ——

Ami   D7   G

NANCY LEE

1.   Of all the wives as e'er you know,
        Yeo ho! lads! ho! Yeo ho! yeo ho!
     There's none like Nancy Lee, I trow,
        Yeo ho! lads! ho! yeo ho!
     See, there she stands an' waves her hands, upon the quay,
     An' eve'ry day when I'm away she'll watch for me,
     An' whisper low, when tempests blow, for Jack at sea;
        Yeo ho! lads! ho! yeo ho!
     The sailor's wife the sailor's star shall be.
     Yeo ho! we go across the sea,
     The sailor's wife the sailor's star shall be,
     The sailor's wife his star shall be.

2.   The harbour's past, the breeze blow,
        Yeo ho! etc.
     'Tis long ere we come back, I know,
        Yeo ho! etc.
     But true an' bright, from morn till night, my home will be,
     An' all so neat, an' snug an' sweet, for Jack at sea,
     An' Nancy's face to bless the place, an' welcome me;
        Yeo ho! etc.

3.   The bo's'n pipes the watch below,
        Yeo ho! etc.
     Then here's a health afore we go,
        Yeo ho! etc.
     A long, long life to my sweet wife, an' mates at sea;
     An' keep our bones from Davy Jones, where'er we be,
     An' may you meet a mate as sweet as Nancy Lee;
        Yeo ho! etc.

Written in 1876, this song sold over 70,000 copies in England alone in the first eighteen months of its life. Its rather idealised view of the sailor's wife must have appealed strongly to the Victorians who saw in the life of their own Queen a similar constancy to her husband.

Stephen Adams, the composer, had a lot of success with his sea songs. Among others he wrote 'The Midshipmite', 'The Tar's Farewell' and 'They All Love Jack'. Fred E. Weatherly was probably the most prolific lyricist of all time. When he wrote his autobiography in his seventy-fifth year he noted that he had written literally thousands of songs some 1500 of which were published. Among his well-known lyrics were those for 'Danny Boy', 'Roses of Picardy' and 'The Old Brigade'.

BRISTOL CITY

Words and music: Traditional

Allegro moderato

1. As I walked thro' Bris-tol Ci - ty, I heard a fair maid sing, In be - half of her sail - or, her

BRISTOL CITY

1. As I walked through Bristol City, I heard a fair maid sing,
    In behalf of her sailor, her country and her king;
    And oh, she sang so sweetly, and so sweetly sang she;
    "Oh! of all the sorts of a Colin, why a sailor for me!

2. You may know my jolly sailor, wheresomede'er he does rove,
    He's so neat in his behaviour, and so true to his love;
    His teeth are white as ivory, his cheeks like the damask rose,
    So you may know my jolly sailor, wheresomede'er he goes.

3. For you sailors are men of honour, and men of courage bold,
    If they go to fight their enemies they are not to be controul'd;
    If they get on board a man of war where the thundering cannons roar,
    They venture their lives for gold, and spend it freely on shore."

(Sailor's answer)

4. "Come, come, my pretty Polly, come sit thee down by me,
    For now my pretty Polly, you and I will agree;
    For my Polly is an angel, all dress'd in willow green,
    And she be like any lady, or a beautiful queen.

5. Pretty Poll has got a colour like the roses in June,
    And she plays upon the hipsicols a melodious fine tune;
    Her lips are red as rubies, her eyes as black as sloes,
    So you may know my pretty Polly wheresomede'er she goes.

6. I'll build my love a castle on yonder high ground,
    Where no lord nor yet a monarch can e'er pull it down;
    For the King he can but love his Queen, and my dear I can do the same;
    And you shall be my shepherdess, and I'll be your dear swain."

This charming song was originally inscribed 'A favourite ballad, sung by Mr Huttley, at the convivial societies of Bath and Bristol.' It gives a very idealised picture of a sailor who really does seem to be as gallant as his Polly believes. He is the very model of a devoted lover. One can't help feeling that her talented playing of the 'hipsicols' may have won him over!

A-ROVING

Words: Traditional

Composed by THOMAS HEYWOOD [arr. A. M.]

A-ROVING

1.   In Plymouth Town there lived a maid.
Bless you young women!
In Plymouth Town there lived a maid.
O mind what I do say!
In Plymouth Town there lived a maid,
And she was mistress of her trade.
I'll go no more a-roving with you, false maid.

CHORUS   A-roving, a-roving,
Since roving's been my ruin,
I'll go no more a-roving with you, false maid.

2.   I took this fair maid for a walk.
Bless you young women!
I took this fair maid for a walk.
O mind what I do say!
I took this fair maid for a walk,
And we had such a loving talk.
I'll go no more a-roving with you, false maid.

CHORUS   A-roving, a-roving, etc.

3.   I took her hand within my own.
Bless you young women!
I took her hand within my own.
O mind what I do say!
I took her hand within my own
And said "I'm bound for my old home."
I'll go no more a-roving with you, false maid.

CHORUS   A-roving, a-roving, etc.

4.   In Plymouth Town there lived a maid.
Bless you young women!
In Plymouth Town there lived a maid.
O mind what I do say!
In Plymouth Town there lived a maid,
And she was mistress of her trade.
I'll go no more a-roving with you, false maid.

CHORUS   A-roving, a-roving, etc.

Thomas Heywood's *The Rape of Lucrece* was played in London in about 1630 and contains a tune unmistakably akin to that of 'A-Roving'. It was certainly extremely popular at the time and was presumably taken on board by sailors and used as a capstan or heaving shanty. The words have been rewritten several thousand times by those with an eye for sobriety rather than authenticity. But somehow the original intentions of those ancient singers is never quite sublimated.

THE ANCHOR'S WEIGH'D

Written by SAMUEL JAMES ARNOLD

Composed by JOHN BRAHAM

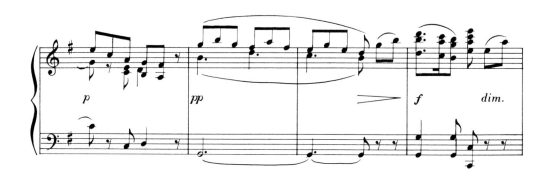

1. The tear fell gen – tly from her eye

G   C   G

When last we part-ed on ___ the shore; My bo-som heav'd with

ma-ny a sigh, To think I ne'er might see ___ her more, To

think ___ I ne'er might see ___ her more. "Dear

youth," she cried, "and canst thou haste a-way? ___ My heart will break, a

lit-tle mo-ment stay; A las, I can-not, I can-not part from thee." "The

an - chor's weigh'd, _____ the an - chor's weigh'd _____ fare-

-well! fare-well! re - mem - ber me."

THE ANCHOR'S WEIGH'D

1. The tear fell gently from her eye
   When last we parted on the shore;
   My bosom heav'd with many a sigh,
   To think I ne'er might see her more.
   "Dear youth," she cried, "and canst thou haste away?
   My heart will break, - a little moment stay;
   Alas, I cannot, I cannot part from thee."
   "The anchor's weigh'd, the anchor's weigh'd,
   Farewell! farewell! remember me."

2. "Weep not, my love," I trembling said,
   "Doubt not a constant heart like mine;
   I ne'er can meet another maid
   Whose charms can fix that heart like thine!"
   "Go, then," she cried, "but let thy constant mind
   Oft think of her you leave in tears behind."
   "Dear maid, this last embrace my pledge shall be!
   The anchor's weigh'd, the anchor's weigh'd,
   Farewell! farewell! remember me."

John Braham (see page 138) sang in the first performances of Weber's *Der Freischutz* and *Oberon* and caused a furore wherever he appeared. Even his sternest critic, Sir Walter Scott, had to admit that although he was 'a devil of an actor' he was 'an angel of a singer'.

'The Death of Nelson' (page 129) was undoubtedly his most popular song and it was his stock encore on almost every musical occasion. His other sea songs, however, were also enormously loved, as J. C. Byrne remembers:

'The great singer knew his public and that he would not be let off without one of his popular songs; the orchestra struck up " 'Twas in Trafalgar's Bay" and even before he had opened his lips the very symphony was applauded to the echo. This spirited and pathetic song touched the hearts of the audience and their shouts for a second encore were so persistent that it was in vain the singer tried to pacify them with bows and smiles. No - it was a marine audience, and a sea song they were determined to have... Whatever Braham's intention may have been, there was nothing for it but compliance.'

One of the best known of Braham's sea songs, 'The Anchor's Weigh'd', is typical of the Georgian songs that were so much in vogue in the early part of the nineteenth century. Sensitively sung, it can still be very effective and, unlike many of Braham's songs, it does not rely on the composer's own rendering to make it palatable.

The words were written by Samuel James Arnold – a dramatist who was responsible for many musical productions in the early nineteenth century both at the Haymarket and Drury Lane. He was also the author of 'The Death of Nelson'.

THE GIRLS AROUND CAPE HORN

Words and music: Traditional [arr.A.M.]

1. The fam'd ship Ca - li - for - ni - a, a ship of high re -
nown, She lay in Bos - ton harbour, 'long side of that pret - ty
town, A - wait - ing for our or - ders to

THE GIRLS AROUND CAPE HORN

1. The fam'd ship *California*, a ship of high renown,
   She lay in Boston harbour, 'longside of that pretty town,
   A-waiting for our orders to sail far from home,
   And our orders came for Rio, boys, and then around Cape Horn.

2. When we arrived in Rio we lay there quite a while,
   A-fixing up our rigging and mending our sails in style,
   From ship to ship they cheer'd us as we did sail along,
   And they wish'd us pleasant weather while rounding of the Horn.

3. While rounding of Cape Horn, my boys, fair nights and pleasant days
   Next place we dropp'd our anchor was in Valparaiso Bay,
   Where those Spanish girls they did roll down, I solemnly do swear
   They far excel those Yankee girls with their dark and wavy hair.

4. They love a Yankee sailor when he goes on a spree;
   He'll dance and sing and makes things ring, and his money he'll spend free,
   And when his money it is all gone on him they won't impose;
   They far excel those Liverpool girls who will pawn and steal his clothes.

5. Here's a health to Valparaiso along the Chile main,
   Likewise to those Peruvian girls, they treated me so fine.
   If I ever live to get paid off, I'll sit and drink till morn
   A health to the dashing Spanish girls I met around Cape Horn.

A favourite song of American sailors in the past, 'The Girls around Cape Horn' is set to a tune that has more than a hint of the Irish folk song about it. It is interesting that the actual rounding of The Horn seems to hold none of its usual terrors... 'Fair nights and pleasant days'. Perhaps the poet, like the sailors, wanted to get to the girls in Valparaiso Bay!

TO ALL YOU LADIES NOW ON LAND

Written by CHARLES SACKVILLE, Earl of Dorset   Composed by JOHN WALL CALLCOTT

1. To all you la-dies now on land We men at sea in-dite, But first would have you un-der-stand How hard it is to write; The Mu-ses now, and

Nep - tune too, we   must im - plore to   write to you, to   write to

D   A   E   A   B

CHORUS

you.   With a   fa   la   la   la   la   la la   With a

E   A   E   A   E

fa   la   la   la   la   la la   With a   fa la la la la   With a

A   E   A   D

fa la la la la   With a   fa la la la la   la   la.

A   D   E   A

TO ALL YOU LADIES NOW ON LAND

1. To all you ladies now on land
   We men at sea indite,
   But first would have you understand
   How hard it is to write;
   The Muses now, and Neptune too,
   We must implore to write to you.

   With a fa la la la la la la etc.

2. In justice you cannot refuse
   To think of our distress,
   When we for hopes of honour lose
   Our certain happiness.
   All these designs are but to prove
   Ourselves more worthy of your love.

   With a fa la la la la la la etc.

3. And now we've told you all our loves,
   And likewise all our fears,
   In hopes this declaration moves
   Some pity for our tears:
   Let's hear of no inconstancy,
   We have enough of that at sea.

   With a fa la la la la la la etc.

Whether Dr Callcott, the composer of this catchy little tune, ever seriously expected hard-headed tars to sing fa-la-las is open to some doubt! Callcott had a nice line in glees and catches in the late eighteenth and early nineteenth centuries when such pieces were very much in demand. His compositions won him a great reputation and many prizes.

Charles Sackville, Earl of Dorset, wrote the words in the late seventeenth century at the time of the first Dutch War. Pepys mentions the song in his diary: 'To my Lord Brounker's by appointment, in the Piazza, Covent Garden; where I occasioned much mirth with a ballet I brought with me, made from the seamen at sea to the ladies in town.' Pepys tune was actually different. It lacked the roistering quality of Callcott's later part song.

BLOW THE WIND SOUTHERLY

Words and music : Traditional

1. Blow the wind south-er - ly, south-er - ly, south-er - ly,

Blow the wind south o'er the bon - ny blue sea.   Blow the wind souther - ly,

south-er - ly, south-er - ly,   Blow bon-ny breeze my lo-ver to me.

They told me last night there were ships in the of-fing, And

Ab   Eb   Fmi7   Bb7   Eb   Eb7

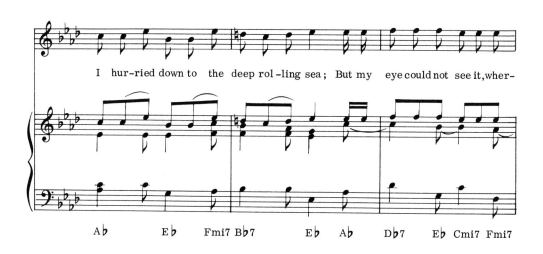

I hur-ried down to the deep rol-ling sea; But my eye could not see it, wher-

Ab   Eb   Fmi7 Bb7   Eb   Ab   Db7   Eb Cmi7 Fmi7

-e'er it might be,— The bark that is bear-ing my lo-ver to me.

Bbmi7 Eb7 Ab7   Ab7   Db   Eb7   Ab

BLOW THE WIND SOUTHERLY

1. Blow the wind southerly, southerly, southerly,
   Blow the wind south o'er the bonny blue sea.
   Blow the wind southerly, southerly, southerly,
   Blow bonny breeze my lover to me.
   They told me last night there were ships in the offing,
   And I hurried down to the deep rolling sea;
   But my eye could not see it, where'er it might be,
   The bark that is bearing my lover to me.

2. Blow the wind southerly, southerly, southerly,
   Blow the wind south that my lover may come.
   Blow the wind southerly, southerly, southerly,
   Blow bonny breeze and bring him safe home.
   I stood by the lighthouse that last time we parted,
   Till darkness came down o'er the deep rolling sea;
   And I no longer saw the bright bark of my lover.
   Blow bonny breeze and bring him to me.

3. Blow the wind southerly, southerly, southerly,
   Blow the wind south o'er the bonny blue sea.
   Blow the wind southerly, southerly, southerly,
   Blow bonny breeze my lover to me.
   Is it not sweet to hear the breeze singing
   As lightly it comes o'er the deep rolling sea?
   But sweeter and dearer by far when 'tis bringing
   The bark of my true love in safety to me.

One of the most beautiful of all the English folk songs, 'Blow the Wind Southerly' comes from Northumberland and was made famous by Kathleen Ferrier's unforgettable rendering of it. The critic of the *Los Angeles Times* commenting on her performance of the song unaccompanied in a recital there in 1950 referred to it as a 'little technical tour de force'. Few singers have Miss Ferrier's technique but anyone can enjoy singing this love song to a sailor.

BLACK-EYED SUSAN

Written by JOHN GAY   Composed by RICHARD LEVERIDGE

Andante ma non troppo

1. All in the Downs ___ the fleet was moor'd, ___ The streamers

Ami   G

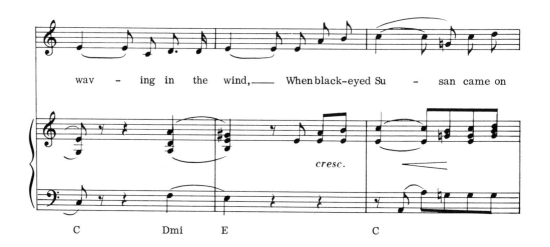

wav — ing in the wind, ___ When black-eyed Su — san came on

C   Dmi   E   C

board___ "O where shall I ___ my true love find? Tell me, ye

jo - vial sail - ors, tell me true, ___ If my sweet

Wil-liam, if my sweet Wil - liam sails a - mong your

crew ?" ___

BLACK-EYED SUSAN

1.   All in the downs the fleet was moor'd,
     The streamers waving in the wind,
     When black-eyed Susan came on board,
     "Oh, where shall I my true love find?
     Tell me, ye jovial sailors, tell me true,
     If my sweet William sails among your crew?"

2.   William was high upon the yard,
     Rock'd by the billows to and fro,
     Soon as her well-known voice he heard,
     He sigh'd and cast his eyes below;
     The cord slices swiftly thro' his glowing hands,
     And, quick as lightning, on the deck he stands.

3.   "Believe not what the landsmen say,
     Who tempt with doubts thy constant mind,
     They'll tell thee sailors, when away,
     In every port a mistress find.
     Yet, yes, believe them when they tell thee so,
     For thou art present wheresoe'er I go.

4.   Oh Susan, Susan, lovely dear!
     My vows for ever true remain,
     Let me kiss off that falling tear,
     We only part to meet again;
     Change as ye list, ye winds, my heart shall be
     The faithful compass that still points to thee."

5.   The boatswain gave the dreadful word,
     The sails their swelling bosoms spread;
     No longer must she stay on board;
     They kiss – she sigh'd – he hangs his head;
     The less'ning boat unwilling rows to land,
     "Adieu," she cries, and waves her lily hand.

The words of this popular song were written by John Gay in about 1720. He was a highly successful writer and is chiefly remembered nowadays for his *Beggar's Opera* (1728). It is interesting how he makes William deny the sailor's most celebrated reputation for having 'a wife in every port'. Black-eyed Susan appears to accept his explanation even though it is a bit literary!

Richard Leveridge was famous for his voice. Apart from singing and composing, he also found time to open and run a coffee shop in Tavistock Street, Covent Garden. His most famous song betrays his interest in things gastronomic – 'The Roast Beef of Old England'.

THE SAILOR'S COMPLAINT

Words: Traditional

Composed by GEORGE A. STEVENS

Moderato

1. Come and lis - ten to my dit - ty, All ye jol - ly hearts of gold; Lend a bro - ther tar your pi - ty, Who was once so stout and bold. But the ar - rows of

THE SAILOR'S COMPLAINT

Come and listen to my ditty,
All ye jolly hearts of gold;
Lend a brother Tar your pity,
Who was once so stout and bold.
But the arrows of Cupid,
Alas! have made me rue;
Sure, true love was ne'er so treated,
As am I by scornful Sue.

When I landed first at Dover,
She appear'd a goddess bright;
From foreign parts I was just come over,
And was struck with so fair a sight.
On shore pretty Sukey walked,
Near to where our frigate lay,

And altho' so near the landing,
I, alas! was cast away.

When first I hail'd my pretty creature,
The delight of land and sea,
No man ever saw a sweeter,
I'd have kept her company;
I'd have fain made her my true love,
For better, or for worse;
But alas! I could not compass her,
For to steer the marriage course.

Once, no greater joy and pleasure
Could have come into my mind,
Then to see the bold *Defiance*
Sailing right before the wind,
O'er the white waves as she danced,
And her colours gaily flew:
But that was not half so charming
As the trim of lovely Sue.

On a rocky coast I've driven,
Where the stormy winds do rise,
Where the rolling mountain billows
Lift a vessel to the skies:
But from land, or from the ocean,
Little dread I ever knew,
When compared to the dangers
In the frowns of scornful Sue.

Long I wonder'd why my jewel
Had the heart to use me so,
Till I found, by often sounding,
She'd another love in tow:
So farewell, hard-hearted Sukey,
I'll my fortune seek at sea,
And try in a more friendly latitude,
Since in yours I cannot be.

The boot is very firmly on the other foot with this traditional sea song. For once it is the sailor who is cast aside while the girl finds another beau. The melody, from the eighteenth century, was composed by George Alexander Stevens.

5

ASLEEP IN THE DEEP

Given to fantasy as he is, the sailor has dreamt up some extraordinary tales, and among the more unlikely products of his imagination is the mermaid. She exists in many nautical traditions around the world, a siren of irresistible appeal but frustrating shape, always ready to lure a man to destruction on the rocks. Thus has the sailor personalised the dangers ever-present in his calling.

No one can know how many have perished at sea. Who can count those who have fallen from the rigging at the height of a storm or been washed overboard and vanished without trace? Not to mention the countless thousands who have died in battle, disappearing without memorial into the wide anonymity of the sea. The oceans have always held nameless terrors, and man has even yet found no way of taming them entirely. So in his songs he has made them bearable by inventing a kind of Shangri-la among the seaweed, a place of peace and quiet dreams where he will be rocked like a baby by the motion of the sea and know release at last from the restless motion of his everyday existence.

Here as in other sections of this book, high-flown artificial sentiment will be found alongside true and unadorned expressions of grief at the loss of a loved one, a loss the more poignantly felt when he has gone to an unmarked grave.

THE MERMAID

Words and music : Traditional [arr.A.M.]

1. On __ Fri - day morn __ when we __ set __ sail, And our

ship not far from the land; We __ there did es-py __ a __

fair__ pret-ty maid with a comb and a glass in her hand, her hand, her hand, with a

CHORUS

comb and a glass in her hand.   For the ra - ging seas_ did _

A7   D   D   A7

roar,   And the stor - my   winds did _ blow,   While

D   G   D

we jol - ly sai -lor boys were up,   up a -loft, And the land - lubbers ly-ing down be-

Bmi   A   G   D   A7

- low, be-low, be-low, And the lands-men were all   down be - low.

D   G   A7   D

THE MERMAID

1. On Friday morn when we set sail,
    And our ship not far from the land;
    We there did espy a fair, pretty maid,
    With a comb and a glass in her hand.

CHORUS For the raging seas did roar,
        And the stormy winds did blow,
        While we jolly sailor boys were up, up aloft,
        And the landlubbers lying down below, below, below,
        And the landsmen were all down below.

2. Then up spoke the captain of our gallant ship,
    And a brave young man was he;
    "I've a wife and a child in fair Bristol Town,
    But a widow I fear she will be."

CHORUS For the raging seas did roar, etc.

3. Then up and spake the little cabin boy,
    And a pretty little boy was he;
    "Oh, I'm more grieved for my daddy and my mam
    Than you for your wife may be."

CHORUS For the raging seas did roar, etc.

4. Then three times round went our gallant ship,
    And three times round went she;
    For the want of a lifeboat, all went down,
    And she sank to the bottom of the sea.

CHORUS For the raging seas did roar, etc.

Mermaids turn up in the folklore of almost every seafaring nation. The attributes of the species vary slightly, but nearly all mermaids are portrayed as having long blond hair which they comb whilst looking at themselves in a mirror. It is, too, always considered bad luck to see a mermaid and in some traditions sailors see mermaids before they die. This popular sea song bears the legend out with a vengeance.

THE WRECK OF THE HESPERUS

Written by HENRY WADSWORTH LONGFELLOW — Composed by JOHN L. HATTON

Allegro

It was the schooner Hes-pe-rus That sail'd in the win-t'ry sea, And the skipper had ta'en his lit-tle daugh-ter to bear him com-pa-ny. Blue

were her eyes, as the fai - ry flax, Her cheeks like the dawn of

day, _____ And her bo - som white as the haw - thorn buds That

ope in the month of May. The skipper he _ stood be -

-side the helm, With his pipe in his mouth, And

watch'd how the veer - ing   flaw did_ blow_ The_ smoke now west, now

south.   Then   up   and spoke an   old   sai - lor, Had

sail'd   the Spa - nish   main,   "I   pray thee, put in - to

yon - der   port, For I   fear   a   hur - ri - cane.   Last

skies;   The lan - tern gleam'd thro' the fal - ling snow On his

fix'd and glas - sy eyes.

ff

dim.   *riten.*

più lento

Then   the   maid - en clasp'd her

pp *più lento*

hands, and pray'd That sav - ed she might be;   And she

thought of Him who still'd the waves On the lake of Gal - li - lee. But fast thro' the mid - night dark and drear, Thro' the whist - ling sleet and snow, Like a sheet - ed ghost, the bark swept on To the reef of "Nor-man's

woe."

sf furioso

Her   rat - tling shrouds, all

sheath'd in   ice, With the   masts went by   the   board;

sf ten.

Like   a   ves-sel   of   glass   she

Andante

At day-break, on the bleak sea beach A fisher-man stood a-

-ghast, To see the form of a maid-en fair Float by on a drift-ing

mast. The salt sea was fro-zen on her breast, The

salt tears in her eyes; And her stream-ing hair, like the

THE WRECK OF THE HESPERUS

1. It was the schooner Hesperus,
    That sail'd in the wint'ry sea,
    And the skipper had ta'en his little daughter
    To bear him company.

2. Blue were her eyes, as the fairy flax,
    Her cheeks like the dawn of day,
    And her bosom white as the hawthorn buds
    Like a vessel of glass she stove and sank,

3. The skipper he stood beside the helm,
    With his pipe in his mouth,
    And watch'd how the veering flaw did blow
    The smoke now west, now south.

4. Then up and spoke an old sailor,
    Had sailed the Spanish Main,
    "I pray thee, put into yonder port,
    For I fear a hurricane.

5. Last night the moon had a golden ring,
    But tonight no moon we see."
    The skipper he blew a whiff from his pipe,
    And a scornful laugh laugh'd he.

6. Down came the storm, and smote amain
    The vessel in its strength;
    She shudder'd and paus'd like a frighted steed,
    Then leap'd her cable's length.

7. "Come hither! come hither! my little daughter,
    And do not tremble so,
    For I can weather the roughest gale
    That ever the wind did blow."

8. "Dear father! I hear the church bell ring,
    Oh say what may it be?"
    "'Tis a fog bell on a rock-bound coast,
    We must steer for the open sea."

9. "Dear father! I see a gleaming light
    O say what may it be?"
    But the father answer'd never a word,
    A frozen corpse was he.

10. Lash'd to the helm all stiff and stark,
    With his pale face to the skies;
    The lantern gleam'd thro' the falling snow
    On his fix'd and glassy eyes.

11. Then the maiden clasp'd her hands, and pray'd
    That saved she might be;
    And she thought of Him who still'd the waves
    On the lake of Galilee.

12. But fast thro' the midnight dark and drear,
    Thro' the whistling sleet and snow,
    Like a sheeted ghost, the bark swept on
    To the reef of 'Norman's Woe'.

13. Her rattling shrouds, all sheath'd in ice,
    With the masts went by the board;
    Like a vessel of glass she stove and sank,
    Ho! Ho! the breakers roar'd!

14. At daybreak on the bleak sea beach
    A fisherman stood aghast,
    To see the form of a maiden fair
    Float by on a drifting mast.

15. The salt sea was frozen on her breast,
    The salt tears in her eyes;
    And her streaming hair, like the brown sea-weed,
    On the waves did fall and rise.

16. Such was the wreck of the Hesperus,
    In the midnight and the snow!
    Oh! save us all from a death like this,
    On the reef of 'Norman's Woe'.

After the horrific wrecking of the schooner *Hesperus* on the reef of Norman's Woe, off Gloucester, Massachusetts in 1839, Longfellow was inspired to write one of his best-known poems. One of the bodies washed ashore was, in fact, lashed to a spar. This gave the poet his theme.

John Liptrot Hatton was mostly self-taught as a musician. He enjoyed an enormous popularity during the nineteenth century for his ballads which are often of the highest quality. He also produced two cathedral services, eight anthems, a mass, an operetta and two operas. He was also well known as a performer, mostly of his own songs, which he interpreted in such a way that he invariably had the audience at his feet.

A good performance of 'The Wreck of the Hesperus' can still be a very moving experience today nearly 150 years after it was first heard.

THE WHITE SQUALL

Written and composed by GEORGE A. BARKER

Allegretto

1. The   sea ___ was
2. They   near'd ___ the

bright ___ and the bark rode well, ___ The breeze ___ bore the
land ___ where in beau - ty smiles, ___ The sun - ny

tone ___ of the Ves - per bell; 'Twas a gal - lant
shore ___ of the Gre - cian Isles; All thought of

bark, ___ with crew as brave, ___ as e - ver
home, of the wel - come dear, ___ Which soon should

launch'd ___ on the heav - ing wave, ___ As e - ver
greet ___ each wan - d'rer's ear, ___ Which soon should

launch'd — on the heav — ing wave. — She shone in the
greet — each wan — d'rer's ear. And in fan - cy —

light — of de - clin — ing day, — And each sail was
join'd — the so - cial throng, — In the fes - tive

set, and each heart — was — gay, She — shone — in the
dance and the joy - ous — song, And — fan - cy

light — of de - clin — ing day, — And each sail was
join'd — the so - cial throng — In the fes - tive

set —— and each heart was gay, —— and each heart ——
dance, —— and the joy - ous song, —— and the joy -

—— was gay. ——
- ous song. ——

3. A white —— cloud glides —— thro' the a - zure sky. —— What

means —— that wild —— des - pair - ing cry? ——

Andante con espressione

Fare-well the vision'd scenes of home! Fare-well the vision'd scenes of

home! That cry is help where no help can come, That cry ___ is

a tempo

help where no help ___ can come! Fare-well the vi-sion'd

ad lib.

scenes of home; Fare-well the vision'd scenes of home!

Allegro

- cean   grave,   in _____ an o -

- cean   grave,   in _____ an o -

- - cean   grave. _____

THE WHITE SQUALL

1. The sea was bright and the bark rode well,
    The breeze bore the tone of the vesper bell:
    'Twas a gallant bark, with crew as brave,
    As ever launch'd on the heaving wave.
    She shone in the light of declining day,
    And each sail was set and each heart was gay.

2. They near'd the land where in beauty smiles
    The sunny shores of the Grecian isles:
    All thought of home, of that welcome dear,
    Which soon should greet each wand'rer's ear.
    And in fancy join'd the social throng,
    In the festive dance and the joyous song.

3. A white cloud glides thro' the azure sky,
    What means that wild despairing cry?
    Farewell, the vision'd scenes of home!
    That cry is Help! where no help can come.
    For the White Squall rides on the surging wave,
    And the bark is gulph'd in an ocean grave.

This typical Victorian naval scene was composed by George A. Barker (1812–1876). Barker was a highly successful writer of ballads and his best-known composition – 'The Irish Emigrant' – is still popular today. 'The White Squall' is full of dramatic moments and really repays a full-blooded rendering.

THE BAY OF BISCAY

Written by ANDREW CHERRY

Composed by JOHN DAVY

Moderato

f

1. Loud

sf

roar'd the dread-ful thun - der, The rain a de-luge show'rs, The _

p

Bb   Eb   C   F

clouds were rent a - sun - der By_ light-ning's vi - vid_ pow'rs. The_

night was drear and dark, Our poor de - vo - ted bark,_ Till next

day there she lay In_ the Bay of_ Bis - cay, O!

THE BAY OF BISCAY

1. Loud roar'd the dreadful thunder,
    The rain a deluge show'rs,
    The clouds were rent asunder
    By lightning's vivid pow'rs.
    The night was drear and dark,
    Our poor devoted bark, –
    Till next day there she lay
    In the Bay of Biscay, O!

2. Now, dash'd upon the billow,
    Her op'ning timbers creak,
    Each fears a wat'ry pillow,
    None stop the dreadful leak.
    To cling to slipp'ry shrouds,
    Each breathless seaman crowds,
    As she lay till next day
    In the Bay of Biscay O!

3. At length the wish'd for morrow
    Broke thro' the hazy sky,
    Absorb'd in silent sorrow,
    Each heav'd a bitter sigh,
    The dismal wreck to view,
    Struck horror in the crew,
    As she lay all that day
    In the Bay of Biscay O!

4. Her yielding timbers sever,
    Her pitchy seams are rent,
    When Heav'n, all bounteous ever,
    It's boundless mercy sent,
    A sail in sight appears,
    We hail her with three cheers,
    Now we sail, with the gale,
    From the Bay of Biscay O!

Andrew Cherry, who wrote the words of 'The Bay of Biscay', was the son of
a printer and bookseller in Dublin. Starting his working life in his father's firm,

he soon left to become an actor – a career in which he had a considerable success. As a writer, he produced many pieces for the stage including the popular *The Soldier's Daughter* which was produced at Drury Lane in 1804 'with much applause'.

The Bay of Biscay was notoriously hard to navigate and because of its diverse currents and numerous inlets was dreaded by sailors who encountered furious storms there. Cherry's song, set in these treacherous waters, however, has a happy ending.

There is a brief biography of John Davy on page 111.

THE SHIP I LOVE

Written and composed by FELIX McGLENNON

Allegretto moderato

1. A gal - lant ship was lab - 'ring

here at my post I'll stand._____ Good - bye, my lads, good-

B   E   A   Dmi   E   Ami

- bye! _____ Good - bye, my lads, good bye! "_____

E   Adim   E   A7

" I'll   stick to the   ship,   lads,   you   save your

mf

D

lives, _____   I've   no - one to   love   me,

A7

you've   chil-dren and   wives; _____   You

E   A7   D

take to the   boats,   lads,   pray-ing to Heav'n a-

A7

-bove, _____   But I'll   go   down in the an-gry

D   G

deep, with the   ship   I   love." _____

                                                    D.C.

A   A7   D

THE SHIP I LOVE

1.   A gallant ship was lab'ring
Lab'ring in the sea;
The Captain stood amongst his crew,
"Gather around," said he.
"This ship is doomed and sinking,
There on the lee is land,
Then launch the boats and pull away,
But here at my post I'll stand.
Goodbye, my lads, goodbye!"

CHORUS   I'll stick to the ship, lads,
You save your lives,
I've no one to love me,
You've children and wives;
You take the boats, lads,
Praying to heaven above,
But I'll go down in the angry deep,
With the ship I love.

2.   The crew stood hesitating,
Their hearts were staunch and true;
With tear-dimm'd eyes spoke up the mate,
"Sir, we will die with you!"
The Captain cried, "What? Mutiny?
I am the captain here!
So launch the boats and pull away,
And think of your children dear.
Goodbye, my lads, goodbye!"

CHORUS   I'll stick to the ship, lads, etc.

This music-hall song was introduced to the great British public by Tom Costello and enjoyed a huge success. The rather perky little tune seems a bit out of place accompanying such a solemn story. One can't help feeling that the composer had the melody in mind for something else.

Felix McGlennon was an Irishman who made a great success as a composer of popular songs in the late nineteenth century. He was not only popular in England, he also had a great following in the United States where, like Mark Twain, he once had the sobering experience of reading his own obituary in the newspapers.

TOM BOWLING

Written and composed by CHARLES DIBDIN

Andante

1. Here, a sheer hulk, lies poor Tom Bow-ling,The dar – ling of our__

crew, _____ No more he'll hear the _ tem - pest how - ling For

death has broach'd him to.   His form was of the _

man - liest beau - ty, His heart was kind and soft! _____

Faithful be - low he did his du - ty, And now he's gone a -

TOM BOWLING

1. Here, a sheer hulk, lies poor Tom Bowling,
   The darling of our crew,
   No more he'll hear the tempest howling
   For death has broach'd him to.
   His form was of the manliest beauty,
   His heart was kind and soft!
   Faithful below he did his duty,
   And now he's gone aloft,
   And now he's gone aloft!

2. Tom never from his word departed,
   His virtues were so rare,
   His friends were many, and true-hearted,
   His Poll was kind and fair:
   And then he'd sing so blithe and jolly,

Ah many's the time and oft!
But mirth is turned to melancholy,
For Tom is gone aloft,
For Tom is gone aloft.

3.   Yet shall poor Tom find pleasant weather,
When He, who all commands,
Shall give, to call life's crew together,
The word to pipe all hands:
Thus death, who kings and tars dispatches,
In vain Tom's life has doff'd,
For though his body's under hatches,
His soul is gone aloft,
His soul is gone aloft!

One of the best known and loved songs in the English language, 'Tom Bowling' was written by Charles Dibdin to honour the memory of his beloved elder brother Tom. Tom was twenty-nine years older than his more famous brother, Charles, and died at sea in India after the vessel of which he was the captain was struck by lightning.

The song, originally known as 'Poor Tom Bowling' achieved an instantaneous popularity and has kept its freshness over the years largely because of the melody which sends Tom's soul winging to heaven at the end of each verse. The last four lines of the first verse were considered appropriate to be carved on Charles Dibdin's own tombstone. There is a biography of Dibdin on page 143.

STORMALONG

Words and music: Traditional [arr. A.M.]

1. O Stor - my he is dead and gone; To my way, you storm a - long. O Stor-my was a good old man; Ay, ay, ay, Mister Storm-a-long.

G   C   C   Ami

E   Ami   Dmi   F   G7   C

STORMALONG

1. O Stormy, he is dead and gone;
   To my way, you storm along,
   O Stormy was a good old man;
   Ay, ay, ay, Mister Stormalong.

2. We'll dig his grave with a silver spade,
    To my way, you storm along,
    And lower him down with a golden chain.
    Ay, ay, ay, Mister Stormalong.

3. I wish I was old Stormy's son,
    To my way, you storm along,
    I'd build a ship of a thousand ton.
    Ay, ay, ay, Mister Stormalong.

4. I'd fill her with New England rum,
    To my way, you storm along,
    And all my shell-backs, they'd have some,
    Ay, ay, ay, Mister Stormalong.

5. O Stormy's dead and gone to rest,
    To my way, you storm along,
    Of all the sailors he was best.
    Ay, ay, ay, Mister Stormalong.

One of the most stately of all sea shanties, 'Stormalong' sums up the sailors' admiration for a great man who has died. It has always been very popular and hardly surprisingly for it has one of the most touching melodies of all.

It is tantalising to speculate who was the original of 'Mister Stormalong'. He must have been quite a character. One authority insists that he was, in fact, John Willis – a famous early-Victorian London ship master and owner whose son was also called John Willis and owned the famous *Cutty Sark*.

ROCKED IN THE CRADLE
OF THE DEEP

Written by EMMA HART WILLARD

Composed by JOSEPH P. KNIGHT

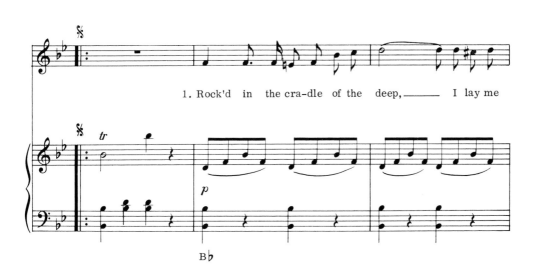

1. Rock'd in the cra-dle of the deep, _____ I lay me

down _____ in peace to sleep. Se - cure, I rest up-on the

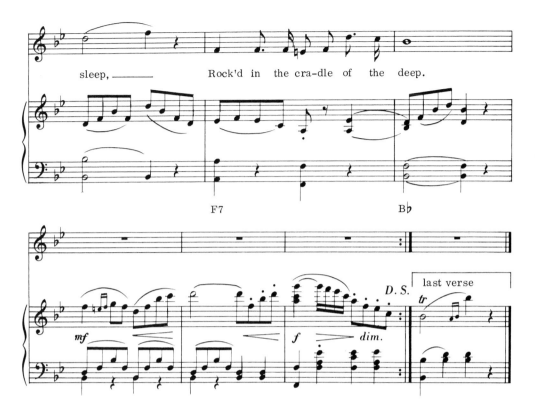

sleep, _____ Rock'd in the cra-dle of the deep.

F7 Bb

D. S. | last verse

mf   f   dim.

ROCKED IN THE CRADLE OF THE DEEP

1. Rock'd in the cradle of the deep,
I lay me down in peace to sleep.
Secure, I rest upon the wave,
For Thou, O Lord, hast power to save.
I know Thou wilt not slight my call,
For Thou dost mark the sparrow's fall,
And calm and peaceful is my sleep,
Rock'd in the cradle of the deep;
And calm and peaceful is my sleep,
Rock'd in the cradle of the deep.

2. And such the trust that still were mine,
Tho' stormy winds swept o'er the brine;
Or tho' the tempest's fiery breath
Rous'd me from sleep to wreck and death,

In Ocean cave still safe with Thee,
The hope of immortality;
And calm and peaceful is my sleep, etc.

Written by Mrs Willard as she crossed the Atlantic on her way home from Europe in 1832, this song soon became a favourite maritime ballad in the setting by Joseph P. Knight. He was for a year a teacher of music in the school in Vermont run by Mrs Willard and it was then that he made his famous setting of her poem. Joseph Knight eventually returned to England and settled down as a clergyman in the parish of St Agnes in the Scilly Isles. Of his 200 or so songs, 'Rocked in the Cradle of the Deep' has survived as the best known.

ASLEEP IN THE DEEP

Written by ARTHUR J. LAMB   Composed by H. W. PETRIE

ASLEEP IN THE DEEP

1. Stormy the night and the waves roll high,
   Bravely the ship doth ride,
   Hark! while the lighthouse bell's solemn cry
   Rings o'er the sullen tide.
   There on the deck see two lovers stand,
   Heart to heart beating, and hand to hand;
   Tho' death be near, she knows no fear
   While at her side is one of all most dear.

CHORUS Loudly the bell in the old tower rings,
   Bidding us list to the warning it brings:
   Sailor, take care! Sailor, take care!
   Danger is near thee, beware! beware!
   Many brave hearts are asleep in the deep, so beware! beware!

2. What of the storm when the night is o'er?
   There is no trace or sign.
   Save where the wreckage hath strewn the shore,
   Peaceful the sun doth shine.
   But when the wild, raging storm did cease,
   Under the billows two hearts found peace,
   No more to part, no more of pain,
   The bell may now tell its warning in vain.

CHORUS Loudly the bell in the old tower rings, etc.

Very much a song for the nautical basso profundo, the words for 'Asleep in the Deep' were written by Arthur J. Lamb, the nineteenth-century lyricist of such music-hall favourites as 'Only a Bird in a Gilded Cage' and 'The Bird on Nellie's Hat'. Although an Englishman, he spent much of his life in America as a successful Tin Pan Alley writer. The composer, Henry Petrie, is probably best known for his children's song – 'I don't want to play in your yard'. This song, however, shows just how deep the roots of music hall were in both men's musical experience. The singer here must be watched as well as heard.

6

WHEN THE BOAT COMES IN

'Home is the sailor, home from the sea.' That is the vision which sustains the seafarer and those who care for him, and it has given rise to numberless poems and songs, ranging from Homer's *Odyssey* to Victorian drawing room ballads such as 'Saved from the Storm'. When the boat safely enters harbour the moment of reunion comes for lovers – and for children, a time of long-promised pleasures denied them while their father is away earning the necessary cash. Even though landfall may, for the sailor, lead to disappointment and ultimately to the desire to set sail once more, he thinks of it as the object of his voyage and the fulfilment of his dreams.

It is this aspect of the sailor's life which has appealed most strongly to the evangelist. The incessant motion of his existence provides the perfect simile for the errant human soul whose ultimate haven is some great Harbour in the sky, and Victorian song writers in particular made constant use of this convenient parable. One can't help thinking that the refuge they had in mind bore a strong resemblance to the front parlour, with its roaring fire, antimacassars and heavy plush curtains, tightly drawn to exclude any draught from the evil world outside.

Whether as the subject of a drawing-room ballad or roughly-fashioned folk song, the sailor in all the aspects of his life has brought home a rich store of words and music, and all of us, whether we go to sea or not, have enough in common with the sailor's temperament to enjoy them thoroughly.

SAVED FROM THE STORM

Written by FRED. E. WEATHERLY

Composed by ODOARDO BARRI

It was a Bre-ton vil-lage, that lay by the sea ____

She was a fish-er - maid - en, Ma - ri-ner stout was he; ____ Fare-

-well, true heart, for   we   must part, The wind cal - ling down the

sea.   But for   me   thou'lt pray in the cha - pel   grey

Na - vi-tas Sal - va   Do - mi - ne,   Na - vi-tas Sal - va,

Do -   mi   - ne.

col canto

f

Bright was the Bre - ton vil - lage, Bright, bright was the

sea; ____ She was a fish - er - mai - den,

Ma - ri - ner stout was he. 'Twas Heav'n a - bove That

rall.   a tempo   e mezza voce

a tempo   col canto

saved me,— love! And brought me back from storm to thee; In the

cha - pel grey We'll kneel and pray, Glo – ri – a ti – bi

Do - mi – ne, Glo – ri – a ti –bi,— ti – bi

Do – mi–ne.

SAVED FROM THE STORM

1. It was a Breton village, that lay by the sea,
She was a fishermaiden, Mariner stout was he;
Farewell, true heart, for we must part,
The wind calling down the sea.
But for me thou'lt pray in the chapel gray
Navitas Salva Domine.

2. It was a night of terror, wild was the sea,
He in the storm is drifting, watching in prayer is she,
Sweet heart! Sweet heart! and must we part?
No boat can live in such a sea,
But still she cries with streaming eyes,
Navitas Salva Domine.

3. Bright was the Breton village, bright was the sea;
She was a fishermaiden, Mariner stout was he.
'Twas Heav'n above that sav'd me, love!
And brought me back from storm to thee;
In the chapel gray we'll kneel and pray,
Gloria Tibi Domine.

Italian names have always been fashionable in the musical world and many composers have adopted Italianate pseudonyms. Odoardo Barri might not have done nearly so well if he had stuck to his real name – Edward Slater. Barri (1844–1920) is probably best remembered for his immensely popular 'The Old Brigade' – a song in which he once again collaborated with Fred E. Weatherly. 'Saved from the Storm' is typical of the late nineteenth-century drawing-room ballad – three verses in an almost nocturne-like structure based on a simple harmonic progression with quasi-religious undertones in both words and music. It must have been extremely well received with its polite whiff of salty spray – enough to entertain, without disturbing one leaf of the aspidistra.

THE PILOT

Written by THOMAS HAYNES BAYLY

Composed by SIDNEY NELSON

1. "Oh, Pi - lot,'tis a fear - ful night, There's danger on the

A   D

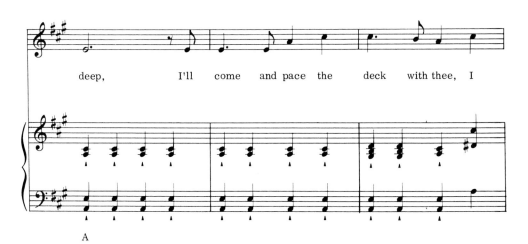

deep, I'll come and pace the deck with thee, I

A

do not_ dare_ to sleep." "Go down," the sai - lor_

E   B   E

cried, "go down, This is no place for_ thee.___ Fear

A   D   A   Bmi   E

not! but trust in Pro - vi-dence, Where - ev - er thou may'st

A   E

be."

A

THE PILOT

1. "Oh! Pilot! 'tis a fearful night,
   There's danger on the deep,
   I'll come and pace the deck with thee,
   I do not dare to sleep."
   "Go down," the sailor cried, "go down,
   This is no place for thee;
   Fear not! but trust in Providence,
   Wherever thou mayst be."

2. "Ah! Pilot, dangers often met
   We all are apt to slight,
   And thou hast known these raging waves
   But to subdue their might."
   "It is not apathy," he cried,
   "That gives this strength to me,
   Fear not but trust in Providence,
   Wherever thou mayst be.

3. On such a night the sea engulphed
   My father's lifeless form;
   My only brother's boat went down
   In just so wild a storm;
   And such, perhaps, may be my fate,
   But still I say to thee,
   Fear not but trust in Providence,
   Wherever thou mayst be."

Thomas Haynes Bayly was a society poet who flourished at the beginning of the nineteenth century. He had some considerable success despite his critics who were many and articulate. However, a poet who can pen lines like:

> 'I'd be a butterfly born in a bow'r,
> Where roses and lilies and violets meet;
> Roving for ever from flower to flower,
> And kissing all buds that are pretty and sweet:'

can't be all bad! Certainly his 'Pilot' is made of sterner stuff.

Sidney Nelson, the composer, lived and died in London in the early nineteenth century. He wrote over 800 pieces, chiefly ballads, among which the best known were 'The Better Land' and 'Mary of Argyle'. In later life he arranged a musical and dramatic entertainment with members of his family and toured America, Canada and Australia.

WHEN THE BOAT COMES IN

Words and music: Traditional [arr.A.M.]

1. Come here, maw lit-tle Jack-y,
Now aw've smoked mi backy, Let's hev a bit o' crack-y, Till the boat comes in.

Dance ti thy dad-dy, Sing ti thy mam-my, Dance ti thy dad-dy,

Ti thy mam - my sing.   Thou shalt hev a fish - y

C   D   G   G

On a lit - tle dish-y,   Thou shalt hev a fish - y   when the boat comes in.

C   D   G   C   D   G

WHEN THE BOAT COMES IN

1. Come here, maw little Jacky,
   Now aw've smok'd mi backy,
   Let's hev a bit o' cracky,
   Till the boat comes in.

CHORUS   Dance ti' thy daddy, sing ti' thy mammy,
         Dance ti' thy daddy, ti' thy mammy sing;
         Thou shall hev a fishy on a little dishy,
         Thou shall hev a fishy when the boat comes in.

2. Here's thy mother humming,
   Like a canny woman;
   Yonder comes thy father,
   Drunk – he cannot stand.

CHORUS   Dance ti' thy daddy, sing ti' thy mammy,
         Dance ti' thy daddy, ti' thy mammy sing;

Thou shall hev a fishy on a little dishy,
Thou shall hev a haddock when the boat comes in.

3.   Our Tommy's always fuddling,
He's so fond of ale,
But he's kind to me,
I hope he'll never fail.

CHORUS   Dance ti' thy daddy, sing ti' thy mammy,
Dance ti' thy daddy, ti' thy mammy sing;
Thou shall hev a fishy on a little dishy,
Thou shall hev a bloater when the boat comes in.

4.   I like a drop mysel',
When I can get it sly,
And thou, my bonny bairn,
Will lik't as well as I.

CHORUS   Dance ti' thy daddy, sing ti' thy mammy,
Dance ti' thy daddy, ti' thy mammy sing;
Thou shall hev a fishy on a little dishy,
Thou shall hev a mackerel when the boat comes in.

5.   May we get a drop,
Oft as we stand in need;
And weel may the keel row
That brings the bairns their bread.

CHORUS   Dance ti' thy daddy, sing ti' thy mammy,
Dance ti' thy daddy, ti' thy mammy sing;
Thou shall hev a fishy on a little dishy,
Thou shall hev a salmon when the boat comes in.

One of the best-loved of all Northumbrian folk songs, 'When the Boat Comes In' is perhaps as well known under its alternative title 'Dance to your Daddy'. The subject – the fisherman/father's return from the sea – is heavily laced with references to alcohol . . . so heavily in fact that one gets the impression that the whole family is incapable! R. R. Terry in his collection, *Salt Sea Ballads*, finds the verses 'all very silly and witless, and a libel on the Northumbrian fisher folk'. We prefer to see it rather more in terms of 'a bit o' cracky' – just a bit of fun!

THE TIGHT LITTLE ISLAND

Written and composed by THOMAS DIBDIN

Moderato

Dad-dy

Nep-tune one day— to Freedom did say,— "If ev-er I live up-on

dry land, The spot I should hit on would be lit-tle Bri-tain," Says

Freedom,"Why that's my own Is - land." Oh! what a snug lit-tle

Is - land, A right lit-tle, tight lit-tle Is - land!

All the globe round, none can be found So hap-py as this lit-tle Is - land.

THE TIGHT LITTLE ISLAND

1. Daddy Neptune one day to Freedom did say,
    "If ever I live upon dry land,
     The spot I should hit on would be little Britain."
    Says Freedom, "Why that's my own Island."
    Oh! what a snug little Island,
    A right little, tight little Island!
    All the globe round, none can be found
    So happy as this little Island.

2. Julius Caesar, the Roman, who yielded to no man,
    Came by water, he couldn't come by dry land;
    And Dane, Pict and Saxon, their homes turn'd their backs on,
    And all for the sake of our Island,
    Oh, what a snug little Island,
    They'd all have a touch at the Island;
    Some were shot dead – some of them fled,
    And some stay'd to live in the Island.

3. Then a very great war-man, called Billy the Norman,
    Cried "Hang it! I never liked my land;
    It would be much more handy to leave this Normandy,
    And live on yon beautiful Island."
    Says he, "'Tis a snug little Island,
    Shan't us go visit the Island?"
    Hop, skip and jump, – there he was plump,
    And he kick'd up a dust in the Island.

4. Yet party deceit helped the Normans to beat,
    Of traitors they managed to buy land;
    By Dane, Saxon, or Pict, we ne'er had been lick'd,
    Had they stuck to the King of the Island,
    Poor Harold, the King of the Island,
    He lost both his life and his Island;
    That's very true – what could he do?
    Like a Briton he died for his Island.

5. Then the Spanish Armada set out to invade a,
    Quite sure if they ever came nigh land;
    They couldn't do less than tuck up Queen Bess,
    And take their full swing in the Island.

Oh! the poor Queen and the Island,
The drones came to plunder the Island,
But snug in her hive, the Queen was alive,
And buzz was the word in the Island.

6. These proud, puffed-up cakes thought to make ducks and drakes,
    Of our wealth: but they scarcely could spy land,
    Ere our Drake had the luck to make their pride duck,
    And stoop to the lads of the Island.
    Huzza! for the lads of the Island;
    The good wooden walls of the Island;
    Devil or Don, let 'em come on,
    But how'd they come off at the Island!

7. I don't wonder much that the French and the Dutch
    Have since been oft tempted to try land,
    And I wonder much less they have met no success,
    For why should we give up our Island?
    Oh! 'tis a wonderful Island,
    All of 'em long for the Island;
    Hold a bit there, let'em take fire and air,
    But we'll have the sea and the Island.

8. Then since Freedom and Neptune have hitherto kept tune
    In each saying, "This shall be my land
    Oh the Army of England to all they could bring land,
    Would show'em some play for our Island.
    We'd fight for our right to the Island,
    We'd give'em enough of the Island;
    Invaders should just – bite at the dust
    But not a bit more of the Island.

Thomas John Dibdin was the second of two illegitimate sons of the great Charles Dibdin, the composer of 'Tom Bowling'. Both boys were brought up by a rich uncle under their mother's name, Pitt, although they later assumed the name of their famous father and were both involved in composition and playwriting for Sadlers Wells and Covent Garden. Tom was born in 1771 and was apprenticed to a London upholsterer. He ran away, however, to Eastbourne where he started on his theatrical career. Of his 2000 or so songs and 200 operas and plays, it is probably 'The Tight Little Island' from his show *The British Taft* (1797) that is best remembered today. Tom Dibdin's career, like his father's, had its financial ups and downs. He lost everything through his own mismanagement of the Surrey Theatre in 1822 but survived until 1841.

PULL FOR THE SHORE!

Written and composed by PHILIP PAUL BLISS

1. Light in the darkness, sailor, day is at hand!

See o'er the foam-ing bil-lows fair Ha – ven's land.

Drear was the voy-age, sai-lor, now al-most o'er;

PULL FOR THE SHORE

1.   Light in the darkness, sailor, day is at hand!
    See o'er the foaming billows fair Haven's land.
    Drear was the voyage, sailor, now almost o'er;
    Safe within the lifeboat, sailor, pull for the shore.

CHORUS   Pull for the shore, sailor, pull for the shore!
    Heed not the rolling waves, but bend to the oar;
    Safe in the lifeboat, sailor, cling to self no more!
    Leave the poor old stranded wreck and pull for the shore!

2.   Trust in the lifeboat, sailor; all else will fail.
    Stronger the surges dash and fiercer the gale,
    Heed not the stormy winds, though loudly they roar;
    Watch the 'bright and morning star' and pull for the shore.

CHORUS   Pull for the shore, sailor, etc.

3.   Bright gleams the morning, sailor, uplift the eye;
    Clouds and darkness disappearing, glory is nigh!
    Safe in the lifeboat, sailor, sing evermore,
    "Glory, glory, hallelujah!" Pull for the shore.

CHORUS   Pull for the shore, sailor, etc.

Nineteenth-century evangelists were fond of using the sea as an image of life. Hymn books of the period are full of references to the Ship of Faith tossed on the foaming billows while anxious sailors ask themselves whether their anchors will hold. Sankey and Moody's famous collection – *Sacred Songs and Solos* – is no exception to the rule. In the stirring choruses, Christians are constantly being exorted to 'Throw out the Lifeline' and to 'Cross the Bar', guided, naturally, by the Great Pilot.

Philip Paul Bliss was typical of gospel hymn-writers of the time. He had, though, more 'hits' than many – such numbers as 'Hold the Fort' and 'Free from the Law' as well as the immensely popular 'Pull for the Shore'. Born in northern Pennsylvania of poor parents he spent a barefoot childhood but began to arouse interest when he displayed musical precocity. A meeting with Dwight L. Moody in 1839 convinced Bliss that his life and talent should be dedicated to God. He became a tireless singer and composer of hymns writing some seven books of them and singing to congregations at Dr Whittle's revival rallies across America.

ANCHORED

Written by SAMUEL K. COWAN

Composed by MICHAEL WATSON

Fly - ing, with flow - ing sail, O-ver the sum - mer sea!

Sheer thro' the seeth-ing gale, Home-ward bound was she! ____

Fly - ing with feath'-ry prow, Bounding with slant-ing keel ____ And

glad ____ and glad was the sai - lor lad, ____ As he

steer'd ____ and sang at ____ his

wheel. _____ "On - ly an - o - ther day to

stray, _____ On - ly an - o - ther night to

roam, _____ Then safe _____ at last, _____ the

har - bour past, Safe in my fa - ther's

home, _____ Safe _____ in my fa- ther's home! " _____

Bright on the flash-ing brine, Glit-ter'd the sum-mer sun!

Sweet - ly   the   star - ry shine   Smil'd   when   the   day   was done !

Blithe ___ was the breeze of Heav'n,   Fil - ling the fly - ing   sail, ___   And

glad   was   the   sai - lor lad, As he   steer'd ___ and   sang   thro' the

gale. _____   "On - ly an - o -ther day to   stray, ___

On - ly an - o - ther night to roam, _____ Then

safe ___ at last, ___ the har - bour past, Safe in my

fa - ther's home, _____ Safe _____ in my

fa - ther's home ! "

Agitato

Sud-den the light-nings flash'd,   Like   fal - chions in the

mf

dark!   Sud-den the thun-ders crash'd!   A -

cresc.

cresc.   *f*   *f*

molto rall.   **Andante**

- las! for the gal - lant   bark!   There when the storm had   pass'd,   A

sf   *p*   *p*

drea - ry wreck lay she! But bright was the star - ry light, That

shone on the sum-mer sea! And a soft smile came from the

stars, And a voice from the whisp - 'ring

foam. Safe, safe at last, the

ANCHORED

1.   Flying, with flowing sail,
    Over the summer sea!
    Sheer thro' the seething gale,
    Homeward bound was she!
    Flying with feath'ry prow,
    Bounding with slanting keel
    And glad was the sailor lad,
    As he steer'd and sang at his wheel.

CHORUS   'Only another day to stray,
    Only another night to roam,
    Then safe at last, the harbour past,
    Safe in my Father's home!"

2.   Bright on the flashing brine,
    Glitter'd the summer sun!
    Sweetly the starry shine
    Smil'd when the day was done!
    Blithe was the breeze of heav'n,
    Filling the flying sail,
    And glad was the sailor lad
    As he steer'd and sang thro' the gale.

CHORUS   "Only another day to stray, etc.

3.   Sudden the lightnings flash'd,
    Like falchions in the dark!
    Sudden the thunders crash'd!
    Alas! for the gallant bark!
    There when the storm had pass'd,
    A dreary wreck lay she!
    But bright was the starry light,
    That shone on the summer sea!

4.   And a soft smile came from the stars,
    And a voice from the whisp'ring foam.
    Safe, safe at last, the danger past,
    Safe in his Father's Home!

When the temperance movement was at its height, it was often seafaring themes that were used as parables in song. The particular brand of muscular Christianity that characterised the Victorian ethic found its most natural expression in the nautical ballad in which the sea was taken as an image of life. Heaven was the safe harbour and between birth and death the young sailor on the sea of life was buffeted by storms and often almost wrecked.

Michael Watson was a ballad composer with a particularly fine line in sea songs. 'Anchored', though, was his most successful. 'The Times' reported in amazement that it had realised £1212.15.0 – 'the largest price, we believe, that has ever been given for a song'. It certainly repays a bravura performance with its stirring chorus and final safe arrival in the straights of Paradise.

CROSSING THE BAR

Written by ALFRED, LORD TENNYSON

Composed by
CHARLES HUBERT HASTINGS PARRY

1. Sun — set and eve - ning star, And one clear call for

me! And may there be no moan - ing of the

bar, When I put out to sea. But

such a tide as mov - ing seems a - sleep, too

full for sound and foam When that which drew from out the bound-less

deep Turns a - gain home.

CROSSING THE BAR

1.   Sunset and evening star,
     And one clear call for me!
     And may there be no moaning of the bar,
     When I put out to sea,
     But such a tide as moving seems asleep,
     Too full for sound and foam,
     When that which drew from out the boundless deep
     Turns again home.

2.   Twilight and evening bell,
     And after that the dark!
     And may there be no sadness of farewell,
     When I embark;
     For tho' from out our bourne of Time and Place
     The flood may bear me far,
     I hope to see my Pilot face to face
     When I have crost the bar.

Charles Hubert Hastings Parry (1848–1918) – one of the best-loved English composers – is probably best remembered today for his setting of Blake's poem 'Jerusalem'. His career was as distinguished as it was successful and honours were poured upon him by a nation grateful for such state anthems as 'Blest Pair of Sirens' and 'I was glad when they said unto me'. In 1894 he became Director of the Royal College of Music and he was created a baronet in 1903. In the same year his setting of Tennyson's famous poem 'Crossing the Bar' was composed and was heard for the first time at the Hereford Festival. Since then it has found its way into countless hymn books and collections of inspirational songs where its Edwardian grandeur is quite at home.

Parry's prolific output and apparent facility were the envy of many of his contemporaries, some of whom doubtless gave credence to the apocryphal story of his being called away to interview a prospective student at the Royal College of Music and, thrusting a manuscript he was working on onto the desk of a secretary, said: 'Carry on with this for a few bars, I'll be back shortly!'

TOM'S GONE TO HILO

Words and music: Traditional [arr. A.M.]

SOLO

1. Tommy's gone, and I'll go

CHORUS

too, A - way down Hi - lo, _____ Oh, Tommy's

gone, and I'll go too, Tom's gone to Hi - lo. _____

TOM'S GONE TO HILO

1.   Tommy's gone, and I'll go too,
CHORUS Away down Hilo,
       Oh, Tommy's gone, and I'll go too,
CHORUS Tom's gone to Hilo.

2.   Tommy's gone, what shall I do?
CHORUS Away down Hilo,
       Oh, Tommy fought at Trafalgar,
CHORUS Tom's gone to Hilo.

3.   Tommy fought at Trafalgar,
CHORUS Away down Hilo,
       Oh, Tommy fought at Trafalgar,
CHORUS Tom's gone to Hilo.

4.   The Old Vict'ry led the way,
CHORUS Away down Hilo,
       The brave Old Vict'ry led the way,
CHORUS Tom's gone to Hilo.

5.   Tommy's gone for evermore,
CHORUS Away, down Hilo,
       Oh, Tommy's gone for evermore,
CHORUS Tom's gone to Hilo.

Hilo is one of those names that turns up again and again in sea songs and it is hard to say just what it means – is it some kind of Nirvana for honest tars? One version of this song gives an answer. The second verse reads: 'Hilo town's in Old Peru ...' This must mean the town of Ylo (always pronounced 'High-Low') which was captured by the buccaneer Bartholomew Sharp in 1681.

At any rate, 'Tom's Gone to Hilo' is one of the most beautiful of all the halliard shanties. The sad thing is that in practice, the lines are just a little too long for optimum productivity. That is to say, if it is sung in proper time, there is too much singing in between hauls – something that was not appreciated by ship-owners. Nevertheless, 'Tom's Gone to Hilo' has survived intact as one of the most popular of all the shanties.

INDEX OF SONGS